RETHINKING
AMERICAN
INDIAN
HISTORY

RETHINKING AMERICAN INDIAN HISTORY

Edited by Donald L. Fixico

UNIVERSITY OF NEW MEXICO PRESS
ALBUQUERQUE

Library of Congress Cataloging-in-Publication Data

Rethinking American Indian History / edited by Donald L. Fixico.—1st ed.
        p.   cm.
Includes bibliographical references (p.   ) and index.
ISBN 0-8263-1819-3 (pbk. : acid-free paper)
    1. Indians of North America—Historiography. 2. Ethnohistory—United
States. 3. United States—Historiography. I. Fixico, Donald Lee, 1951—
E76.8.R47   1997
973'.0497'0072—dc21   94-4745
                                                                            CIP

For Keytha John Fixico,
whose generation will have
a better understanding of American Indians

Contents

Preface

This book of essays on thinking about and writing American Indian history began as ideas for annual conferences to address the scholarship dealing with Native Americans.

As of this date, four conferences have been held, and the two most recent addressed the scholarship about American Indians. These two conferences were "New Scholarship About the West and American Indians" (1994) and "Methodologies and American Indian History" (1995). The conferences were funded by the administration at Western Michigan University, and made possible by the efforts of several people.

Certain people helped to fund these conferences, including President Diether Haenicke, former Provost Nancy Barrett, former Dean Douglas Ferraro of the College of Arts and Sciences, and Dr. Ronald Davis, chairperson of the History Department. They have encouraged the studies of American Indians at the university and have been supportive of my efforts to bring increasing attention to Western Michigan University since I arrived six years ago.

Key individuals have played important roles in planning and working at these conferences and are to be thanked for their efforts. These special people include David Anthony, now at Northern Arizona University; Professor Linda Robyn, also at Northern Arizona University; Michelle Martin Figueroa; and Eva Martinez. A special thanks is for the graduate students in the History Department and the History Graduate Student Organization. In particular, Mary Younker, Barbara Sears, Rob Galler, Kevin Vichcales, April Summitt, Charles Johnson, Deborah Blain, Jim Shiley, and others are to be thanked for finding extra time to help with the conferences. Two key people, who can always be depended upon for last-minute help and on a daily basis are Alberta Cumming and Lori Klingele of the History Department. I would also like to thank the students of the Native American Student Organization.

I am also grateful to Deborah Tucker of the Purdy/Kresge Library at Wayne State University, Detroit.

Also, I want to thank David Holtby of the University of New Mexico Press for being supportive of this book project. He has always been supportive of my work and has always listened to my ideas about American Indian history. In this same light, I appreciate the support of Ronald Davis and Douglas Ferraro. People who have influenced my thinking about and teaching of American Indian history without their realization include Blue Clark, the late Angie Debo, R. David Edmunds, the late Arrell M. Gibson, Laurence Hauptman, Reginald Horsman, Fred Hoxie, Peter Iverson, H. Wayne Morgan, Floyd O'Neil, Donald Parman, and Gregory Thompson. I also want to thank the contributing authors—James Axtell, William T. Hagan, Theda Perdue, Glenda Riley, Richard White, and Angela Cavender Wilson— for making time to participate in the conferences and for writing their essays within the context of methodology and Native American history.

Important people who have sacrificed time, and to whom I am always thankful, are my wife, Dr. Sharon O'Brien Fixico, and our new son, Keytha. My time working on this project took precious time from them. I hope that this book will be of important use to all people interested in American Indians.

DONALD L. FIXICO
Western Michigan University

RETHINKING
AMERICAN
INDIAN
HISTORY

Introduction

This book is for individuals who are interested in thinking about American Indian history. Specifically, the history of Native Americans as a field has entered a new era during this generation of scholars. The complexity of Native American life and the various cultures and languages of more than five hundred Indian nations have challenged scholars to reconsider carefully previous views and interpretations in the writing of American Indian history. In trying to reconstruct the Indian past, current scholars are utilizing innovative analytical theories and cross-disciplinary methods in their writing of Native American history. The essays in this volume focus on some of these various methodologies and theoretical trends, and demonstrates how the scholarship of this field has drastically changed.

Earlier scholars and writers wrote colorfully about bloody Indian wars or courageous native patriots fighting to save their people. Whether they depicted Indians as "good guys" or "bad guys"—and mostly as the latter—scholars and writers wrote "about" Native Americans as vividly as possible in a descriptive genre. This simple narrative approach of interpreting non-Indian generated documents about Indians, along with surreal imagination, accounted for more than thirty thousand books written about American Indians with roughly 90 percent written by non-Indians.

Today's studies about American Indians take into consideration the facts and factors as well as different sources of research data. How and why this new scholarship occurred are the concerns of this book of essays on the status of American Indian history as a field to be studied, as well as of the various analytical ways of examining the field.

The enormous complexity of American Indian life has caused scholars to pause and to rethink their work. To rethink Native American history is to use new theories and methodologies, and introducing this revisionist approach is the purpose of this book. This volume of essays is the result of two conferences, held in 1994 and in 1995 at Western Michigan University as a part of the annual American Indian studies conference series. The 1994 conference was entitled "New Scholarship about the West and American Indians," and the conference in 1995 featured "Methodologies and American Indian History."

Two papers from the "New Scholarship" conference, by William T. Hagan and Glenda Riley, help constitute Part 1 of this volume on historiography in American Indian history. The first essay is by James Axtell, Kenan Professor of Humanities at the College of William and Mary. His essay, entitled "The Ethnohistory of Native America," conveys the viewpoint of a colonial historian who writes about the ethnohistorical relations of colonial–Indian relations. Intrigued with eastern Native Americans and their communities, Axtell described the evolution of ethnohistory as a field and identified his interest as including the vital role of Native Americans in his vision of colonial America. He found himself listening to anthropologists and reading their works in a frustrating attempt to understand native roles. Because a workable definition of ethnohistory was needed, Axtell had to apply his own definition, that "ethnohistory involved the use of historical and ethnological methods and materials to gain knowledge of the nature and causes of change in culture [or cultures] defined [ethnologically]."[1] Axtell reminds us that perceiving cultures as a whole, with all their social parts and interacting subcodes in order, is imperative for understanding their realities. This social analysis of historical cultures would also include examining historical and ethnological materials in reconstructing the past. Using this approach means employing William Fenton's theory of "upstreaming," or working retroactively from reliable ethnographic observations among modern native descendants, as opposed to "downstreaming," or working with the flow of time.[2] Although ethnohistory has some imperfections, Axtell argues that it is "the sharpest, most comprehensive, most inclusive, most flexible tool we have for writing and teaching the history of America's native peoples."[3]

Also stressing the contribution of ethnohistory, William T. Hagan, professor of history at the University of Oklahoma, includes western history in the emergence of American Indian history. In fact, in contrast to Axtell's eastern version of colonial–Indian relations, Hagan speaks from the western historian's point of view, and proceeds to cover the historiography of American Indian history through his observation of books that represent the rise of Native American history and how it has changed. Following in the footsteps of a newly emerged and debated "New Western History," Hagan describes the development of a "New Indian History." In his essay, "The New Indian History," Hagan traces the historiographic development of this history, which emerged from ethnohistory. The collaboration of the disciplines of history and anthropology in the 1960s yielded ethnohistory as a cross-disciplinary interest in American Indian cultures. Hagan argues that this led afterward to a burgeoning status for American Indian history today. Tribal history has enticed younger scholars to enter the field in increasing numbers as another generation begins to ponder topics for their first publications and dissertations. Simultaneously, tribal history, environmental history, ethnohistory, biographical history, and modern Indian history has attracted younger scholars to the field. How this "New Indian History" flourished from its roots in ethnohistory, and has been influenced by western history, is the focus for Hagan, who primarily does western Indian history. He also identifies the trends and the scholarly contributions of "The New Indian History" in his essay.

From another western historian's viewpoint, Glenda Riley, Alexander M. Bracken Professor of History at Ball State University, provides a study of Indian women's historical literature and demonstrates how it has been influenced by women's history. In her essay, "The Historiography of American Indian and Other Western Women," Glenda Riley has identified several significant trends of the literature about native women and women's historical literature. Her observations are based on the premise that the female gender is central to the creation of Indian life at symbolic and physical levels. Although women's history is a recently emerged field, Riley contends that it initially overlooked Indian women. But in order to understand the fullness of Indian life largely in regard to social and cultural development, one can use techniques in women's history for interpreting the seemingly invisible, ever-present roles of native women in American Indian societies. Riley says that Turnerian and frontier historians managed to include western white women in the categories of "pioneer" and "settler," but finally the scholarship of the 1960s and 1970s began to raise more interest in western women's history, which provided the entry to American Indian women's history.

A growing interest during subsequent decades in studies of women of color and in multiculturalism yielded studies of the image of Indian women and the stereotypes surrounding them. The interest in myth was greater than that in the reality of native women, until the mid-1980s established women's history as well as a lasting scholarly interest in Indian women. In stages of scholarly attention focusing on women's history, and then on women of color, a rising interest in American Indian women's history has become clear. Indian women's biographies, Native American gender, and an overlap with other women's histories, especially in the West where the environment separated the genders of men and women, has marked a literary interest in studying native women's history. Yet, as Riley contends, the West forced men and women to work together, whether in a white community or in an Indian village, and the ever-present role of Indian women can be effectively studied via studying women's history.

The geographic division of North America, largely accomplished by making the Mississippi River the line separating the eastern half of the country from its western half, has been aided by environmental differences. Climate, spatial differences, moisture levels, and varying species of flora and fauna and their populations, all the result of natural elements, have heavily influenced a division of eastern and western historians. Naturally, this division can be further subdivided into other regional distinctions, but a striking difference is observable between eastern scholars and western scholars who study Native American Indian history.

The essays in Part 2 of this book deal with "analysis" and "methodologies" in American Indian history. From an eastern scholar's viewpoint and stressing women's history as a tool, Theda Perdue, professor of southern history at the University of Kentucky and an authority on southeastern Indian history, provides an essay that is a geographic counterbalance to Glenda Riley's essay. In "Writing the Ethnohistory of Native Women," Theda Perdue addressed the dire need of history and anthropology to resolve the absence of women in Native American history. This neglect is due to the gender problem of men writing history and of Indian men being perceived as the major players in Indian history. Unmistakably, the germane influence of women is fundamentally integral to understanding Indian history properly. Basic differences of gender have caused Indian men and women to develop separate economic and societal roles. Understandably, male and female ceremonies developed. Fortunately, women anthropologists began to assert gender as an element in the cultural construction of society, setting aside ethnocentric attitudes about women in order to initiate a revisionary examination of how Indian men and women used languages differently, and to make a study of the social, economic, and political importance of women's rituals and kinship relations. Perdue's call for a comparative analysis of Indian men and women roles invites a new understanding for the male-dominated writing of history to comprehend gender in its multiple contributions in Native American cultural systems.

Physical environment is central in Indian life and Native American history. In his essay, Richard White, McClelland Professor of History at the University of Washington, writes about the importance of environmental history as a research tool, one that must be cautiously used. In "Indian Peoples and the Natural World: Asking the Right Questions," Richard White warns us about the confusion of methodology with asking proper scholarly questions. He asks two fundamental questions: 1) "How do we know what Indians thought about nature, and what equivalent or related conceptions of the natural world might Indian peoples have had at various times in the past?," 2) "How do we know how Indians acted in the past in regard to the natural world, and what were the consequences of their actions?" In response to these inquiries and in his essay, White says that ethnohistory, environmental history, and environmental sciences are utilized, but with exploratory caution. But we should recognize that we must first deal with our assumptions about Indians. Scholars need to identify basic concepts about the Indian's natural world. White suggests a methodology of rethinking "accepted" terminology such as "Indian," "tribe," and "traditional," and asking operational questions in order to better understand American Indians. Finally, White warns us that while interpreting history we should consider the origin of documented sources and how whites and Indian people perceive their realities and terminology. Additionally, we should be aware of linguistic meanings of terms and question basic previous assumptions, so that a "misreading" of Indians will not continue. Knowing the distance between constructing historical cultures and historical documents is important. In the process, scholars will need to look to other disciplines in pursuit of a scientific investigation of how Indians did things, which would provide additional understanding of their actions in historical events. But in doing so, White reminds us about learning to ask the proper questions before using "interdisciplinary history."

Reconstructing the Indian point of view or recovering the Indian voice is the concern of Angela Cavender Wilson, a doctoral student in history at Cornell University. Angela Wilson argues the validity of oral history in her essay, "Power of the Spoken Word: Native Oral Traditions in American Indian History." In order to write Indian history, one should consult Indian sources, which includes Indian oral history. Wilson cautions scholars to differentiate between oral history and oral tradition. Those people belonging to an oral tradition offer an enriched source of knowledge from a native perspective, according to Wilson, and this is how they record history. For a greater understanding of Indian communities, Wilson suggests that learning the native language would be beneficial, and listening to the elders would be useful in placing the white man's version of Indian history and the Indian versions of Indian history in their proper perspectives. Oral tradition means much more to Indian people, as Wilson, who is Dakota, observes with regard to Dakota history, for it is an integral part of their lives, filled with protocol, conceptionalization, an explanation of the known and the unknown, and it presents a different reality when viewed from inside their communities.

The final essay, "Methodologies and Reconstructing Indian History," is by Donald L. Fixico, professor of history at Western Michigan University. This bibliographic essay is designed to identify current methodologies that are used and some that are not used by scholars in writing Native American history. The complexity of Native American life has finally convinced scholars to look closer at native cultures and their communities as the first proper step in studying Indian history. But what methodologies are being used? And who has used such ideas and different kinds of analytical interpretations in the work they have published? This essay discusses a selection of such work because it would be impractical to say that it is a complete survey of the literature, nor does it include all imaginable methodologies being used in rethinking and writing a new Indian history.

In using innovative theories and methodologies in rethinking American Indian history, the scholars here, whose backgrounds are both white and Indian and of various institutional training in history, have set about to challenge previous, early scholarship about Native Americans and their communities. This new version of rethinking American Indian history must be accomplished in order to reconstruct a true picture of the historic realities of tribal nations and their cultures. Rather than writing "about" American Indians, the generation of scholars represented by those included in this volume seek to understand the dynamics of exchange between Indians and whites, as well as the inside narrative of Indian communities, in forming a new history, in addition to attempting to understand history from an Indian point of view. All this, perhaps, can be done by utilizing the same historical documents and examining new evidence that had been previously neglected, and including a wider range of factors that influenced and shaped American Indian history. It is the primary purpose of this book of critical essays on scholarship and methodology to be of use to serious students of American Indians and those individuals wanting a better understanding of Native Americans and their realities.

Notes

1. James Axtell, "Ethnohistory: An Historian's Viewpoint," *Ethnohistory* 26:1 (Winter 1979), 1–13; repr. in Axtell, *The European and the Indian: Essays in the Ethnohistory of Colonial North America* (New York, 1981).

2. William N. Fenton, *American Indian and White Relations to 1830: Needs and Opportunities for Study* (Chapel Hill, 1957), 21–22.

3. See n. 1.

Part 1
Historiography

1

The Ethnohistory
of Native America

James Axtell

Thirty years ago, when I was entering the academic profession, very few historians pursued the history of America's native peoples. Certainly no historians I knew felt particularly guilty for leaving Indian peoples out of their courses and books, for implying that America *had* no history until the advent of scribbling Europeans and that, even *after* 1492, Indians had little to do with the making of American society and culture generally. Indians (the collective generic was invariably used) and their so-called history were relegated to the Anthropology Department, where odd men in plaid shirts and dirty boots attended to all the "primitive others of the world, who constituted, at best, exotic footnotes to the real history of "civilized" movers and shakers.

Those who were interested in the history of native America, primarily anthropologists, relied almost exclusively on the methodology or investigative procedure known as ethnohistory. So, in 1970, when I belatedly realized that I could not make any sense of colonial America or of the later United States without understanding the role of their native peoples, I turned to scholars who identified themselves as ethnohistorians and convened annually at meetings of the American Society for Ethnohistory. I was drawn initially to that organization because its journal, *Ethnohistory*, published most of the best articles on Indian history I could find in those dim off-line days. (The *American Indian Quarterly* and the *American Indian Culture and Research Journal*, remember, were not founded until 1974 and 1976 respectively.) Some articles, I noticed with interest, were even written by people with degrees and positions in history. In the course of attending those relatively small and friendly meetings and reading the journal, I began to get some feel for the theoretical and operational characteristics of ethnohistory, for what it could do well and what its blind spots were.

As I began to include the Indians in my courses, I felt that I needed at least a working definition of ethnohistory, partly to answer in my own mind the voiced and unvoiced questions some of my more traditional colleagues had about introducing such a novel subject to the curriculum. When I turned to the official statement of the society's aims on the inside front cover of its journal, I found three successive definitions that were not very helpful. Initially, ethnohistory was corporately defined as "original research in the documentary history of the culture and movements of primitive peoples, and related problems of broader scope."[1] In 1966 that definition—at once restricted, demeaning, and hopelessly vague—was replaced by another that was not much better. Ethnohistory, it said, was devoted to "general culture history and process, and the specific history of peoples on all levels of sociocultural organization, emphasizing that of primitives and peasantries, in all world areas."[2] By the winter of 1971 the society's growing sensitivity to nomenclature erased the pejorative reference to "primitives and peasantries" and replaced it with a kinder but equally problematic "non-industrial peoples."[3] Nor would I have been much helped by subsequent definitions. By 1982 ethnohistory had become simply, and confusingly, "the cultural history of ethnic peoples throughout the world."[4] And from 1984 to 1986, when the frustrating official attempt to define the field finally ceased altogether, the society said that its purview was "the past of cultures and societies in all areas of the world, emphasizing the use of documentary and field materials and historiographic and anthropological approaches."[5]

The last definition at least had a familiar ring, because in 1979 I had tried my own hand at defining the field, in part to sort out the different styles and emphases as well as the commonalties of its anthropological and increasingly numerous historical practitioners. To some extent, my characterization of ethnohistory tried to reach a consensus among the many earlier definitions that had been offered by exemplary practitioners such as anthropologists William Fenton, William Sturtevant, Nancy Lurie, Robert Carmack, and Charles Hudson and historian Wilcomb Washburn.[6] But I also wanted to emphasize its distinctive interdisciplinary methods and to avoid the bland vagueness of the society's earlier definitions. As I saw it—and largely still see it—ethnohistory involves "the use of historical and ethnological methods and materials to gain knowledge of the nature and cause of change in a culture [or cultures] defined [ethnologically]."[7]

In probing what such a definition does and does not say, we note first that any culture of any complexity or size anywhere in the world is a potential object of ethnohistorical attention. While the American society and its journal began with an exclusive interest in the native peoples of North America and have since maintained a strong interest in them, nothing about the operating procedures of ethnohistory mandates that it restrict itself to the tribal peoples of the Americas or, indeed, to *tribal* peoples at all. As the journal's articles have shown, particularly in the last fifteen years, ethnohistory is perfectly capable of shedding light on the cultural history of state societies, industrialized societies, colonizing societies, and capitalist societies in regions all over the globe—Africa, Asia, Australia, Europe, and the Americas, North, South, and Central. The group or region studied is much less important than *how* it is studied and with what organizing *focus.*

Ethnohistory, like most workaday anthropology, takes as its most proper subject *culture* as opposed to *society* or socioeconomic organization per se.While sociologists and dictionary makers have little trouble agreeing on what constitutes a society, anthropologists have always had a devil of a time defining culture. When I went to the literature in search of a consensual definition, I quickly realized that I would have to concoct my own from many different strands and theoretical strains. What I came away with was a notion that culture is "an idealized pattern of meanings, values, and norms differentially shared by the members of a society, which can be inferred from the non-instinctive [or learned] behavior of the group and from the symbolic products of their actions, including material artifacts, language, and social institutions."[8] In other words, culture is a kind of code by which a people live and which gives meaning, direction, and order to their lives. The code is an idealized construct, imagined or seen in its entirety and complexity perhaps only by a perceptive and diligent outside observer, because the insiders assume or internalize much of the code during their education or enculturation and because different members of the society are privy only to certain parts of the total code, those most appropriate to their particular class, race, status, gender, age, education, ancestry, family position, region, and so forth.

According to such a definition, ethnohistorians must try mightily to see cultures *whole*, as all of their social parts and sub-codes interact functionally and symbiotically to produce a single cultural organism, which is potentially knowable and translatable to members of other cultures. This is somewhat easier to do, of course, the smaller the society, which explains why ethnohistory has habitually focused on the cultures of relatively small-scale, allegedly "simple" societies, particularly tribal societies. Like all students of "otherness," ethnohistorians must also try to understand each culture, initially at least, on its own terms, according to its own cultural code, because that is the only way to understand *why* people in the past acted as they did. Unless we know what they imagined reality to be and their own particular place and role in it, we will never succeed in re-creating the world they really lived in. For as Charles Horton Cooley, the great early-twentieth-century sociologist, reminded us, society—and he might have said culture too—is "an interweaving and interworking of mental selves. . . . The imaginations which people have of one another are the solid facts of society."[9]

This means that the ethnohistorian must take virtually nothing for granted about the social culture under study if he or she wishes to get inside the heads, to break the code, of its constituent members. Students of a historical culture must start from the premise that "the past is a foreign country; they do things differently there."[10] And not just *some* things, but *everything*, beginning with speaking and thinking. Ideally, every ethnohistorian would enter his or her historical country like a child newly born to the natives, through the slowly forming template of language—oral, mental, and bodily. If the descendants of one's historical subjects and their ancient tongue survive, the ethnohistorian would do well to learn that tongue while becoming acquainted with the other aspects of the culture's past and present. But many scholars study groups whose native languages have been partially or completely lost to change and death, and other scholars do not specialize in a single group but explore larger regions, usually across several linguistic boundaries, so the entry to culture via language is partly closed to them. They can and should, however, seek as much access to the epistemology, ontology, and mental universe of their subjects as possible through historical dictionaries, word lists, and grammars and through some familiarity with the grammatical and syntactical principles and operations of languages belonging to the same linguistic family or cognate groups. This will ensure that they do not unconsciously intrude their own mental prospects and processes upon the very different realms and reasonings of their historical subjects.

In addition to language, ethnohistory draws upon an unlimited host of "historical and ethnological materials" to reconstruct the normative codes of past cultures. In theory at least, it was not always so. In the early sixties, both the journal and most theorists described ethnohistory's primary sources as "historical *documents*," by which they meant almost exclusively the written records of literate societies that came in contact with native cultures. Usually the record makers were explorers, colonists, or imperialists who sought and often secured control over, or destruction of, the native peoples. Invariably, their records and observations of the natives reflected their sociopolitical goals and their own cultural biases, thereby refracting or warping to some extent whatever they saw. Despite these evidential drawbacks, the newcomers often left unique and sometimes abundant records of native peoples whose own histories were as fragile as memory and as perishable as sound. While ethnohistorians should always be skeptical of the *interpretations* placed on the natives' words and actions, the outsider's *descriptions* of that behavior are usually indispensable and often trustworthy, if never as thorough or encompassing as one might wish.

One crucial test of reliability of any evidence pertaining to native life, written or otherwise, is to weigh and measure it critically against ethnological knowledge gained from study of the group or similar groups through a variety of methods and materials. It is this new dimension—the critical use of ethnological concepts, materials, and sensitivity to evaluate historical documents—that separates ethnohistory from history proper. For ethnohistorians can bring to bear "special knowledge of the group, linguistic insights, and understanding of culture phenomena," which allow them to utilize written data more fully than the average historian.[11]

At the same time, documentary historians—particularly those who have paid attention to the latest developments in rhetoric, semiotics, and "colonial discourse"—have much to teach ethnohistorians about the contexts, tropes, and discursive strategies that inform any written record.[12] Language always "says" more than it *denotes*, so it is a major job of the document decoder to deconstruct and decipher all of its messages, to listen as well to its silences and static, before giving credence to any one part. So-called facts always come dressed, not naked, and it behooves ethnohistorians to learn to read the sartorial signs as well as they interpret contemporary speech in the contextual grammar of facial, gestural, and body language. Because we are seldom bequeathed evidence of the extraverbal envelope of historical speech, ethnohistorians should pay close attention to the signifying properties of their written evidence in order to maximize the usefulness of its ethnographic contents. When I served on the board of editors of the journal *Ethnohistory* from 1983 to 1990, the major reason I had for rejecting articles—besides literary ineptitude—was lack of any critical appreciation of the limits of historical documents. Too many anthropologists were historically naive and too many historians were ethnologically innocent.

The best way for ethnohistorians to lose their ethnological innocence is to delve into the broadest possible array of evidence left by the group in question, written and nonwritten. If we want to understand the historical culture of an Indian group in colonial North America, for example, we are obviously denied direct access to the people themselves, none of whom are living. Ethnohistorians are no more unfortunate in this regard than other historians whose subjects are also beyond the reach of interview. In fact, students of American Indian cultures are somewhat better off than most historians because they occasionally enjoy three kinds of second-best evidence of life in earlier centuries. Enduring native languages we have already mentioned. Modern native people who speak an ancient tongue still think, to a considerable extent, in ancient ways. Not entirely or consistently, of course, because every language grows and changes with time and circumstance. Modern Mohawk, while it reveals many traditional habits of mind and constructions of reality, nonetheless incorporates innumerable new words and concepts—borrowed from Dutch, French, English, German, and American neighbors—to account for the new worlds the Mohawks found themselves part of in the four centuries since Samuel de Champlain and Henry Hudson.

Even if descendants of our historical subjects no longer speak their traditional language, they frequently provide two other windows into the past. One is enduring cultural customs and ways of living. Like language, these too are subject to internal change and acculturation to external pressures, direct and indirect. It is highly unlikely that an Indian inhabitant of the eastern United States today lives and thinks exactly or even very much like his ancestors did in 1492 or 1607; unless he or she had remained incredibly isolated from the social history of the last four hundred years, and particularly from the accelerated changes of the past half-century, such a person would carry the telltale marks of change and difference that the modern descendant of New England Puritans and Virginia cavaliers inevitably bear. It is not that ancient customs and cultural patterns do not endure; they do. But they seldom survive in pure, timeless forms or in their original, defining contexts. They come encrusted with accretions and diminished by subtractions, so we must devise ways to peel off the later additions from, and restore the missing pieces to, the original. One such way is to consult every written record of a group's cultural practices, from the time we are studying to the present. This can proceed in either direction—"downstream," with the flow of time, or, at William Fenton's suggestion, "upstream," working back from reliable ethnographic observations among modern descendants through the documents to the desired custom or practice.[13] However difficult it proves, the work must be done if we want to recapture historical verisimilitude rather than settle for an anachronistic substitute.

The other window on the past that native descendants can sometimes provide is oral traditions and memories. Not unlike the written and oral memories of literate peoples, these come in three forms: (in the language of Western scholarship) as *myths* involving spiritual beings and culture heroes; as *histories* concerning events important to the collective definition of the group; and as personal *stories* often involving the moral adventures of friends, relatives, or total strangers. But like cultural customs, oral memories are all subject to change and selective amnesia. So they too must be subjected to critical analysis and cross-checked against other reliable evidence.[14]

Myths provide unique glimpses of native concepts of reality, time and space, causation, planes of existence, cosmologies, and pantheons; but like any part of a growing cultural organism, they can change, thereby altering, perhaps critically, the version we are seeking that was current at a particular time and place. Native oral histories are also keys to our understanding of the natives' understanding of the world they fashioned and inhabited. But again, as we know from even written—and erasable—histories, every generation has reasons to rewrite or manipulate the past to suit its own needs and circumstances. However tenacious and accurate oral traditions can be, native historians were no less susceptible to those temptations to revise. We simply need to double-check whenever possible.

Moreover, native history was not calibrated to Western calendars; what we would call exact dates are usually missing. Nor was native history immune to the propensity of winners to fashion the story they would like their kinsmen and descendants to hear, rather than a more balanced or "objective" account telling about all parties, all motives, and all sets of actions and reactions. But it usually does convey the emotional resonance of the events for the narrator's ancestral group, and often concrete information that can be recovered in no other way.

The most striking example of unique oral information I have encountered came from a series of Abenaki language tapes collected by the late Gordon Day at the acculturated reserve town of St. Francis in southern Quebec in the late 1950s and early 1960s. In telling stories about the famous raid of Major Robert Rogers and his Rangers upon the French-allied village in 1759, at least two narrators revealed that the villagers had been warned about the raid the night before by one of Rogers's Indian scouts. Many villagers believed the warning and hid themselves and their families in four identifiable locations outside the village. But several villagers disregarded it and continued to celebrate a wedding in the council house. When Rogers struck just before dawn, he caught the unwary asleep and claimed to have killed two hundred, close to the village's whole population. Yet French sources put the dead count at only thirty. The only source in English for this key event in the last intercolonial war—made more famous by Spencer Tracy's portrayal of Rogers in the film version of Kenneth Roberts's *Northwest Passage*—is Rogers's own journal. The conundrum solved by Abenaki oral tradition was how, if Rogers had obliterated the village population (as he thought he had), a large and angry French and Indian army had quickly emerged and chased his ragged forces with lethal efficiency back to New

England. Only the Abenakis knew, and no one bothered to ask them for two hundred years.[15]

We know that the natives of America had a very long history before Europeans arrived to observe and record their lives for posterity, which is why we should no longer use the term "*pre*history" to designate the Indian past before 1492. But if we are interested in reconstructing that "pre*contact* history," we are pretty much dependent on just three sources: largely untestable oral tradition; the science and serendipity of archaeology to uncover its material vestiges; and glottochronology to tell us something about language affiliations, formations, and separations. Each source has serious limitations, but when used together, along with the observations of the earliest Europeans, they often sketch a reliable, if partial, portrait of native culture before Western time and print intruded.

After contact, ironically, our access to native evidence expands exponentially. Artists such as John White, Carl Bodmer, George Catlin, and Father Nicholas Point and, later, photographers such as Edward Curtis and William Henry Jackson have left us indelible visual images of many native individuals, groups, and communities. Although most if not all of these images were staged and composed for purposes that had little to do with the future needs of objectifying historians, they still give us valuable insights into native realities while they alert us to ever-changing Western imaginings and agendas.[16]

The Renaissance penchant for collecting exotica or "curiosities" around the world, including walking souvenirs, soon led to more benign but no less colonialist collections and museums of cultural objectives, of which a few large ones were acquired on a systematic scale. Many artifacts were purchased from native owners or trustees; many others were stolen from graves and other archaeological sites. More recently, evidence of the European goods traded in native villages around the Great Lakes has been salvaged intact from the cold-water rivers where wiry *voyageurs* failed to shoot rapids to save another backbreaking portage.[17] If the artifacts come with good provenience, they are immensely useful in revivifying the historical cultures from which they came. Without the collectors' mania for acquisition, no matter how venal or aggrandizing their motives, we would know much less than we do and immeasurably less than we would like to know about Native American cultures.

One of the well-documented artifacts I am grateful for is a braided prisoner tie dropped by Caughnawaga Mohawk raiders near Fort Massachusetts (modern-day Adams) in August 1746. If the Deerfield Memorial Museum had not acquired and preserved it, I and (in my teenage son's words) the tens of readers of one of my articles would not know that the tie crossed through itself, like a dog choke-chain, and featured a wider, quill-decorated strip around the throat, like a woman's tumpline or burden strap, of which it was undoubtedly a variation. No written descriptions ever conveyed these interesting and, to me, important details.[18]

Another rich source of native history is maps. Predominantly, these are European products created to serve colonial or imperial ends.[19] But when they do not simply leave all signs of native communities, claims, and properties off or transmogrify them into European turf with new names, they may contain good evidence of native towns and territories, place-names, migrations, battles, economic activities, and sacred sites. Even their decorative cartouches or border designs sometimes harbor reliable images and ethnographic details by eyewitnesses. Yet natives, too, drew maps for the newcomers— with fingers or sticks on sand and dirt, on birchbark, skin, and paper with charcoal, paint, or quill pens and ink. Much of their information was incorporated in colonial maps, which were then used to wrest the continent from the natives' obliging hands. Native maps also reveal native thinking because they express distances not in units of uniform, abstract, Euclidean space, but in time traveled by foot or canoe. The University of Wisconsin, Milwaukee, has in progress a large project to inventory, annotate, and reproduce all of the known native maps in North America. And the next volume in the impressive *History of Cartography* series, published by the University of Chicago Press, will be devoted to *Cartography in the Traditional African, American, Arctic, Australian, and Pacific Societies*. Its editor, Malcolm Lewis, is also the head researcher for the Milwaukee project.[20]

About other sources for native history we can be summary. The ecological and geographical alterations wrought by native habitations, farming, and hunting can be read on the ground and in records by keen-eyed students of those fields.[21] Art historians and ethnomusicologists can trace cultural codes and changes in the decorative and utilitarian artifacts and in the dances, songs, and chants of historical peoples. And documentary sleuths can tease still more insights into native life from a broader array of written records. Treaty minutes, legislative records, explorers' journals, missionary reports, and captivity narratives are well known and have more to tell us. But we have yet to derive full benefit from such wayward documents as traders' account books and correspondence; military records; slave auction, indentured servant, and plantation records; court records (local and provincial); and writings, newspapers, and other publications of literate natives, who were either self-taught or educated in colonial schools or apprenticeships. In every category of record, we still have much to learn about the gendered approaches and responses of Native Americans to their worlds.[22]

As attractive, challenging, and useful as ethnohistory may seem from my not-disinterested description, it has its critics, not a few of whom are insiders who have used or continue to use its distinctive methodology with signal success. Their criticisms fall into five themes; most object to ethnohistory's name and its implications rather than its goals or procedures.

The first criticism is that although ethnohistory is, in theory, inclusive, it is in practice *exclusionary* because it focuses on small tribal societies, on cultural "Others," and therefore "ghettoizes" their history by calling it by a special polysyllabic and hyphenated name. The ethnohistorical spotlight is seldom turned on large state societies, particularly the colonizing ones that forced themselves upon the world's indigenous peoples to initiate contact. And by effectively relegating native history to a special corner of scholarship, ethnohistory fails to integrate natives into the larger national or global narratives that carry academic weight and inform policymakers.[23] James Merrell, one of its best practitioners, even argues that historians of colonial America were "more sensitive to Indian history in the 1970s, before much of the literature on the subject appeared, than they are today, when the scholarship on Indians is more abundant." This decline he attributes to ethnohistory's "arcane" methodological pretensions, which have scared off most historians, even though many of them pursue similar kinds of multi- or interdisciplinary history of other groups, such as black slaves, indentured servants, women, and sailors.[24]

There is certainly some truth in this criticism. In the twenty years between 1968 and 1987, *Ethnohistory* published 234 articles on American Indians, and only 110 on all other topics.[25] It is also true that ethnohistory *sounds* complicated because it *is* complicated; it requires bifocal, double competencies both in history and anthropology, narrative and analysis, and their constant integration. It is not a field for the lazy or faint-hearted academic entrepreneur looking to pad his or her *vita* or to make an easy mark on the profession. If it takes extra time and effort to achieve competence, I and others would argue that the purchase more than justifies the expense. But I would also admit that ethnohistorians have only just begun to revise the histories of Euro-American colonies and states by viewing their cultures comparatively through the lenses of contiguous native cultures. Bruce Trigger and I have long argued that particularly "the colonial history of Canada and the United States cannot be understood without detailed consideration of the role played by Indians."[26] Wielding a prodigious knowledge of northeastern native cultures, Trigger proceeded to knock Champlain and the Jesuits off their Canadian pedestals, and I wrote a counterfactual scenario of

"Colonial America without the Indians" to demonstrate their utter indispensability to the forging and shaping of its whole history.[27]

Nonetheless, we should also recognize that the colonizers' documentation regarding the natives does and will always outweigh native evidence on the colonizers, and that scholars will understandably, if not forgivably, gravitate to the fattest books and fullest archives. Only those with extra gumption and imagination will try to buck that trend and write colonial history from the "other" side of the frontier.

A variation on the first set of criticisms comes from those who think their academic oxen are being gored by ethnohistorians. In 1982 Harry Porter, a Cambridge don and, in fact, a former tutor of mine, charged the American practitioners of ethnohistory with constituting an exclusive "club," a veritable "church" of self-elected, self-righteous, moralizing snobs who looked down their noses at "mere" historians of Indian–white relations, Western attitudes toward natives, and the West's civilizing mission and accomplishments. Porter's was clearly a cry of wounded chauvinism because he objected strenuously to the "rather irritating anti-English bias" in many ethnohistorians of early America, who seemed to feel duty-bound "to write exposes of the European way of life in America." His pique was not entirely unwarranted: all but two of the twenty-five authors he reviewed were trained historians, who had lived and written in the United States in the turbulent 1970s and who believed that moral judgments deserved a place in ethnohistory. Readers of his essay might have sensed, but could not know for certain, that it was also an unfortunate skirmish in an academic turf fight. Porter dubbed me the "High Priest" of the ethnohistorical communion not only for my recent attempt to define ethnohistory for historians, but because two years earlier I had published a highly critical review of his six hundred–page book, *The Inconstant Savage* (as had three other reviewers), contrasting what I regarded as his unfocused, eccentric approach to intellectual history with the rigor of ethnohistory.[28] Which only shows that new converts to any faith are prone to intolerant enthusiasm and hubris and should guard against them, *especially* when reviewing an old mentor!

A third criticism, now slightly dated, is that ethnohistory's penchant for language about "primitives" is not only "patronizing" but "pernicious," because it abets racist and colonialist attitudes toward other peoples, particularly of color. Africanists in particular warned that reserving the term *ethnohistory* for "people without written history" or who are considered otherwise "primitive" would be highly and rightly resented by the peoples of that complex continent.[29] Since anthropologists in general have largely given up the use of "primitive" as pejorative, misleading, or meaningless, ethnohistorians have followed suit, sometimes opting for substitutes hardly more edifying.[30] "Subalterns" (from Asian historiography) or "peasants" (from Marxism) do not seem destined to sweep the field anytime soon, while "natives" has generic utility only in the early stages of contact, before long-time creoles and colonists earn the right to wear the same label. In the Americas, "Indians" in short, carries no pejorative baggage despite Columbus, and is reasonably clear, unless we do comparative, world, or immigration history, which most ethnohistorians do not.

Objections to the name *ethnohistory* flow in two different directions and constitute a fourth category of criticism. Bruce Trigger, even before his adoption as a Huron, argued that "Native American history" would serve better than the segregating implications of "ethnohistory."[31] But this only compounds the problem by suggesting that the methodology has no other applications than in the Americas, which is clearly not the case. Shepard Krech, the former editor of *Ethnohistory*, prefers "anthropological history" or "historical anthropology" (depending on the slant) for two reasons. One is that the newest and most fruitful histories being written are no less hyphenated than ethnohistory; most disciplines and scholarly genres today are hopelessly "blurred" (in Clifford Geertz's phrase) and happily "osmotic." The second reason is that the bilateral borrowings of method and theory implied by the older definitions of ethnohistory are now being supplied by wider venues of stimulation and challenge. "Theory today is as likely to derive neither, strictly speaking, from anthropology nor history but from semiotics, structuralism, Marxism, critical theory, linguistics, sociology, cultural studies, literary criticism, political economy, or world-system theory—or from some postmodern blend."[32] His point is well taken. While I no longer have a strong attachment to the name except in my teaching of new recruits, I would suggest that most students of Native American history, young and old, are still not greatly influenced by postmodernity and are quite busy enough trying to master two complex disciplines and to gain some bibliographical control—with or without the Internet—over a vast and growing database relating to their subject. If I am right, "ethnohistory" might still retain some usefulness as a denominator of the methodology best designed for the work at hand.

A fifth and final indictment of ethnohistory stems indirectly from a challenge issued by Calvin Martin to all students of Native American cultures. In his edited volume of essays on *The American Indian and the Problem of History*, published in 1987, Martin argued that tribal peoples lived, and perhaps still live, in a mythic world of "biological" time, which is "eternal, cyclical, endlessly repetitive, powered by Nature, and cosmogonic." Western historians cannot hope to comprehend the native worldview unless they use their imaginations to transcend their own limited "linear, remorselessly historical, profane, and anthropological" sense of time. "We historians," he urged, "need to get out of history, as we know it, if we wish to write authentic histories of American Indians." We, too, need to learn to see ourselves as "cosmic mucilage" connecting humans to animals, plants, and the elements, to rewire our heads with "mythic circuitry," and to write our history in "mythic language."[33]

Martin is onto something important here, but he goes much too far. His remedy entails, as Frederick Turner, another contributor to the volume, admits, "conscious abandonment of our Western view of life and human history," a surrender fraught with chaos."[34] If Western historians were to swallow Martin's prescription, they would somehow cease being Westerners and would become Indianized tribespeople. They would, therefore, be incapable of writing the kind of history that modern audiences turn to for their understanding of the past. By the same logic, in their new mindset, they would be as incapable of understanding the European invaders as any mythic, time bound natives must have been. Silence or profound ignorance seem to be the only alternatives.

The way out of Martin's myopic dilemma is provided by Christopher Vecsey, another contributor, who reminds us that Western history has long inculcated the use of "imaginative double vision." We use deep research and empathy to see other people as they saw themselves, but we also use hindsight and objectifying scholarship to see them as they could not see themselves, as only we can. Thus we achieve historical vision, at once "loving and scrutinizing," for our own human purposes, without needing to commit professional or cultural suicide.[35]

In spite of its acknowledged imperfections, ethnohistory remains, I would argue, the sharpest, most comprehensive, most inclusive, most flexible tool we have for writing and teaching the history of America's native peoples. All of the other approaches in use today are but facets of the ethnohistorical ideal. They need to be pursued with every bit as much care and rigor as does the synoptic methodology. But if ethnohistory can adjust to the new intellectual times—and I have no doubt that it can—it will retain its preeminence in the field. If it becomes more reflexive regarding theory, its moral and political implications, and epistemology, if its practitioners become more critical users of documents and records of every sort as well as more tuned to the ethnological resonance of their contents, I see no reason why it should not flourish for many years to come, even under its old name.

But if it does suffer a name change or an erosion of identity in the fast, new academic market, I would hope that a few diehard ethnohistorians would preserve and reserve its name and methodology for one major subject to which both are uniquely suited. I refer to the entwined histories of natives and newcomers in the constantly shifting, contested, polysemous zones of cultural interaction we sometimes still call frontiers. While it is often difficult to known where or when they begin and, even more, end, we know that America's multicultural history was essentially, in its longest chapters, the story of a complex series of successive and overlapping frontiers. If we want to get that story straight for ourselves and future generations, we had better hold on to the single best instrument we have for uncovering it, particularly if we want to do justice to *all* the participants, not just those who allegedly "won"—or "lost."

Notes

1. *Ethnohistory* 4–12 (1954–1965).

2. Ibid., 13:1–2 (Winter-Spring 1966).

3. Ibid., 18:1 (Winter 1971).

4. Ibid., 29:1–4 (1982).

5. Ibid., 31:1 (1984)–33:2 (1986).

6. See James Axtell, "Ethnohistory: An Historian's Viewpoint," *Ethnohistory* 26:1 (Winter 1979), 1–13, esp. 9, n. 3; repr. in Axtell, *The European and the Indian: Essays in the Ethnohistory of Colonial North America* (New York, 1981), chap. 1.

7. Ibid., 2.

8. Ibid.

9. Charles Horton Cooley, *Life and the Student* (New York, 1927), 201–2.

10. L. P. Hartley, *The Go-Between* (New York, 1954), 3.

11. Nancy Oestreich Lurie, "Ethnohistory: An Ethnological Point of View," *Ethnohistory* 8 (1961), 78–92, esp. 83.

12. See, for example, Hayden White, *Tropics of Discourse: Essays in Cultural Criticism* (Baltimore, 1978); White, *The Content of the Form: Narrative Discourse and Historical Representation* (Baltimore, 1987); Michel de Certeau, *The Writing of History*, trans. Tom Conley (New York, 1988); Greg Dening, "A Poetic for Histories: Transformations that Present the Past," in Aletta Biersack, ed., *Clio in Oceania: Toward a Historical Anthropology* (Washington, D.C., 1991), 347–80; Patrick Williams and Laura Chrisman, eds., *Colonial Discourse and Post-colonial Theory: A Reader* (New York, 1994); Benita Parry, "Problems in Current Theories of Colonial Discourse," *Oxford Literary Review* 9 (1987), 27–58; Edward Said, "Representing the Colonized: Anthropology's Interlocutors," *Critical Inquiry* 15 (1989), 205–25; Rolena Adorno and Walter D. Mignolo, eds., *Colonial Discourse*, in *Dispositio* 14:36–38 (1989); Rene Jara and Nicholas Spadaccini, eds., *1492–1992: Re/Discovering Colonial Writing*, in *Hispanic Issues* 4 (1989); Patricia Seed, "Colonial and Post-colonial

Discourse," *Latin American Research Review* 26:3 (1991), 181–200.

13. William N. Fenton, *American Indian and White Relations to 1830: Needs and Opportunities for Study* (Chapel Hill, 1957), 21–22; Fenton, "Field Work, Museum Studies, and Ethnohistorical Research," *Ethnohistory* 13 (1966), 71–85, esp. 75.

14. Walter J. Ong, *Orality and Literacy: The Technologizing of the Word* (London, 1982); Eric A. Havelock, *The Muse Learns to Write: Reflections on Orality and Literacy from Antiquity to the Present* (New Haven, 1986); Brian Swann, *Smoothing the Ground: Essays on Native American Oral Literatures* (Berkeley, 1983); Arnold Krupat and Swann, *Recovering the Word: Essays on Native American Literature* (Berkeley, 1987); Krupat, *Ethnocriticism: Ethnography, History, Literature* (Berkeley, 1992); William S. Simmons, *Spirit of the New England Tribes: Indian History and Folklore, 1620–1984* (Hanover, N.H., 1986).

15. Gordon M. Day, "Rogers' Raid in Indian Tradition," *Historical New Hampshire* 17 (June 1962), 3–17; Day, "Oral Tradition as Complement," *Ethnohistory* 19:2 (Spring 1972), 99–109.

16. For the colonial period, see the contributions of William C. Sturtevant to *The American Drawings of John White, 1577–1590*, ed. Paul Hulton and David Beers Quinn, 2 vols. (London and Chapel Hill, 1964); Sturtevant, "First Visual Images of Native America," in Fredi Chiappelli, ed., *First Images of America: The Impact of the New World on the Old*, 2 vols. (Berkeley, 1976), 1:417–54; Bernadette Bucher, *Icon and Conquest: A Structural Analysis of the Illustrations of de Bry's Great Voyages*, trans. Basia Miller Gulati (Chicago, 1981); Christian F. Feest, "The Virginia Indian in Pictures, 1612–1624," *Smithsonian Journal of History* 2 (Spring 1967), 1–30; John C. Ewers, "An Anthropologist Looks at Early Pictures of North American Indians," *New York Historical Society Quarterly* 33 (October 1949), 222–34. On nineteenth-century photographers, see Christopher M. Lyman, *The Vanishing Race and Other Illusions: Photographs of Indians by Edward S. Curtis* (New York, 1982), and Joanna Cohan Scherer, *Indians: The Great Photographs that Reveal North American Indian Life, 1847–1929, from the Unique Collection of the Smithsonian Institution* (New York, 1973).

17. Robert C. Wheeler et al., *Voices from the Rapids: An Underwater Search for Fur Trade Artifacts, 1960–73* (St. Paul, 1975).

18. C. C. Willoughby, "Mohawk (Caughnawaga) Halter for Leading Captives," *American Anthropologist* 40 (1938), 49–50.

19. J. B. Harley, "Maps, Knowledge, and Power," in Denis Cosgrove and Stephen Daniels, eds., *The Iconography of Landscape: Essays on the Symbolic Representation, Design and Use of Past Environments* (Cambridge, 1988), 277–312; Harley, "Silences and Secrecy: The Hidden Agenda of Cartography in Early Modern Europe," *Imago Mundi* 40 (1988), 57–76; Harley, *Maps and the Columbian Encounter: An Interpretive Guide to the Traveling Exhibition* (Milwaukee: Golda Meir Library, University of Wisconsin, 1990); Harley, "New England Cartography and the Native Americans," in Emerson W. Baker et al., eds., *American Beginnings: Exploration, Culture, and Cartography in the Land of Norumbega* (Lincoln: 1994), chap. 13; Gregory H. Nobles, "Straight Lines and Stability: Mapping the Political Order of

the Anglo-American Frontier," *Journal of American History* 80:1 (June 1993), 9–35; G. N. G. Clarke, "Taking Possession: The Cartouche as Cultural Text in Eighteenth-century American Maps," *Word and Image* 4:2 (April-June 1988), 455–74.

20. Louis De Vorsey, Jr., "Amerindian contributions to the Mapping of North America: A Preliminary view," *Imago Mundi* 30 (1978), 71–78; De Vorsey, "Silent Witnesses: Native American Maps," *Georgia Review* 46:4 (Winter 1992), 709–26; G. Malcom Lewis, "The Indigenous Maps and Mapping of North American Indians," *Map Collector* 9 (1979), 145–67; Lewis, "Indian Maps," in Carol M. Judd and Arthur J. Rays, eds., *Old Trails and New Directions: Papers of the Third North American Fur Trade Conference* (Toronto, 1980), 9–23; Lewis, "Misinterpretation of Amerindian Information as a Source of Error on Euro-American Maps," *Annals of the Association of American Geographers* 77 (1987), 542–63; Gregory A. Waselkov, "Indian Maps of the Colonial Southeast," in Peter H. Wood, Waselkov, and M. Thomas Hatley, eds., *Powhatan's Mantle: Indians in the Colonial Southeast* (Lincoln, 1989), 292–343.

21. Richard White, "Native Americans and the Environment," in W. R. Swagerty, ed., *Scholars and the Indian Experience: Critical Reviews of Recent Writing in the Social Sciences* (Bloomington, 1984), 179–204; William Cronon, *Changes in the Land: Indians, Colonists, and the Ecology of New England* (New York, 1983); Carolyn Merchant, *Ecological Revolutions: Nature, Gender, and Science in New England* (Chapel Hill, 1989); Timothy H. Silver, *A New Face on the Countryside: Indians, Colonists, and Slaves in South Atlantic Forests, 1500–1800* (New York, 1990); Gary C. Goodwin, *Cherokees in Transition: A Study of Changing Culture and Environment Prior to 1775*, University of Chicago, Department of Geography, Research Paper No. 181 (Chicago, 1977).

22. James Axtell, ed., *The Indian Peoples of Eastern America: A Documentary History of the Sexes* (New York, 1981); Mona Etienne and Eleanor Leacock, eds., *Women and Colonization: Anthropological Perspectives* (New York, 1980); Rayna Green, *Native American Women: A Contextual Bibliography* (Bloomington, 1983); Walter L. Williams, *The Spirit and the Flesh: Sexual Diversity in American Indian Culture* (Boston, 1986); Deborah Welch, "American Indian Women: Reaching Beyond the Myth," in Colin G. Calloway, ed., *New Directions in American Indian History* (Norman, 1988), 31–48; Gretchen M. Bataille and Kathleen M. Sands, *American Indian Women: A Guide to Research* (New York, 1991); Nancy Shoemaker, ed., *Negotiators of Change: Historical Perspectives on Native American Women* (New York, 1995).

23. Shepard Krech III, "The State of Ethnohistory," *Annual Review of Anthropology* 20 (1991), 345–75, esp. 363–64.

24. James H. Merrell, "Some Thoughts on Colonial Historians and American Indians," *William and Mary Quarterly*, 3d ser. 46 (January 1989), 94–119, esp. 113–15.

25. Ibid., 115, n. 96.

26. Bruce G. Trigger, "Indian and White History: Two Worlds or One?" in Michael K. Foster, Jack Campisi, and Marianne Mithun, eds., *Extending the Rafters: Interdisciplinary Approaches to Iroquoian Studies* (Albany, N.Y., 1984), 17–33, esp. 21.

27. Trigger, *Natives and Newcomers: Canada's "Heroic Age" Reconsidered* (Kingston and Montreal, 1985); Axtell, "Colonial America without the Indians: Counterfactual Reflections," *Journal of American History* 73 (March 1987), 981–96, repr. in Axtell, *After Columbus: Essays in the Ethnohistory of Colonial North America* (New York, 1988), chap. 11.

28. H. C. Porter, "Reflections on the Ethnohistory of Early Colonial North America," *Journal of American Studies* 16:2 (August 1982), 243–54, esp. 246, 250. For a counterattack by an English-born historian of early native America, see Colin G. Calloway, "In Defense of Ethnohistory," *Journal of American Studies* 17:1 (April 1983), 95–100. My review of *The Inconstant Savage* appeared in the *Journal of American History* 66 (March 1980), 902–3. Calloway cites the other reviews on 99, n. 13.

29. Krech, "State of Ethnohistory," 363, 364.

30. Francis L. K. Hsu, "Rethinking the Concept 'Primitive,'" *Current Anthropology* 5:3 (June 1964), 169–78.

31. Trigger, "Ethnohistory: Problems and Prospects," *Ethnohistory* 29:1 (1982), 1–19, esp. 11.

32. Krech, "State of Ethnohistory," 350.

33. (New York, 1987), 15, 135, 194, 197, 207.

34. Ibid., 116, 117.

35. Ibid., 126.

2

The New Indian History

William T. Hagan

Since the publication in 1987 of Patricia Nelson Limerick's *The Legacy of Conquest*, there has been renewed discussion of the history of the American West and how that history should be written.[1] Meanwhile, a resurgence of popular interest in the West, and specifically in Indians, has been manifested in a spate of television documentaries and in big-screen features such as *Dances with Wolves* and *Geronimo*.

On the scholarly side, there has emerged what is usually referred to as the New Western History. It might have been called the Yale School, as it consists to a significant degree of individuals who were the products of Howard Lamar's seminar in western history at that university. In 1989, two years after Limerick's *The Legacy of Conquest* appeared, two events produced books that added to the academic debate. First, a symposium at Yale in April honored Lamar for his remarkable contributions to western history, both as a mentor for a very talented corps of students and as an outstanding scholar in his own right. The papers presented at this symposium, including one by Limerick, appeared in a volume entitled *Under an Open Sky: Rethinking American's Western Past*, edited by William Cronon, George Miles, and Jay Gitlin.

Meanwhile, Patricia Limerick, with funding from the National Endowment for the Humanities, put together a symposium that took place in Santa Fe in September of 1989. To the three papers presented at this symposium by Donald Worster, Richard White, and Peggy Pascoe, were added nine others. Collectively they were published as *Trails: Toward a New Western History*, edited by Limerick, Clyde A. Milner III, and Charles E. Rankin. The table of contents revealed that the editors did not believe they were just on the trail of a new western history, but rather that they had arrived. The section including the three papers presented at the conference, plus a new one by Limerick, appeared in the table of contents under the heading, "Trails: The New Western History."

This New Western History had its roots in perspectives common to the 1960s. This led, the preface tells us, to "a more balanced view of the western past. It includes failure as well as success . . . women as well as men; varied ethnic groups and their differing perspectives as well as white Anglo-Saxon Protestants. . . ." The editors also called attention to the "enduring yet dynamic Native American Cultures."[2]

One result of this intellectual ferment has been a vigorous debate among western historians. Also, leading newspapers and national magazines began to take note of the movement, and in scholarly sessions and publications throughout the country the concept of a New Western History was expounded and attacked.

"The Gang of Four" was a derogatory term that a few defenders of the old order assigned to Limerick, Richard White, William Cronon, and Donald Worster, the most conspicuous of the New Western Historians. Limerick responded to this by appearing at a meeting of the Western History Association wearing a T-shirt emblazoned "Gang of 400," a declaration more accurate than that implied by "Gang of Four." The New Western History was gaining supporters.

Despite an unnecessarily snide tone indulged in by a few participants in the debate, overall the controversy has been healthy for western history. It forced many scholars to rethink their approaches to their particular facets of the field, and it suggested a vitality and freshness in western history, an area of study that some critics dismissed as no longer relevant.

As someone who was able to take a longer view of the issue than my younger colleagues—and that was almost all of them—I was somewhat bemused by the controversy. I participated in the first meeting of the Western History Association in 1961, an event celebrated in later years as reviving a dying field. And even further back, in the early 1950s, a movement had gotten underway to rethink the methodology employed in studying Native Americans.

At that time the root cause of revisionism was the greatly increased activity in the field brought on by the need for expert testimony for cases before the Indian Claims Commission. The Newberry Library in Chicago sponsored a conference in March 1952, one attended by anthropologists and historians involved in Indian studies. This meeting was followed by another in Columbus later in the year, which produced the Ohio Valley Historic Indian Conference that would launch a new journal, *Ethnohistory*. The name of the organization would be changed, first to the American Indian Ethnohistoric Conference, and in 1966 to the American Society for Ethnohistory, the title under which it has operated since then.[3]

Regardless of the name, the organization has had significant influence on the study of the American Indian. Although founded by anthropologists and historians brought together by their work with the Indian Claims Commission, anthropologists heavily outnumber members with a history background in the organization. This is not strange given the relative importance the two disciplines have assigned to Indian studies. It has been said that anthropology began in the United States "primarily as the study of the American Indians."[4] In contrast, as late as 1950 no history department in the United States offered Indian history as a major field for graduate students, nor were Indian history courses offered at the undergraduate level. A few people had studied Indian policy, with George Dewey Harmon's *Sixty Years of Indian Affairs: Political, Economic and Diplomatic, 1789–1850* coming out in 1941, followed a year later by Loring Benson Priest's *Uncle Sam's Stepchildren: The Reformation of United States Indian Policy, 1865–1887*. But no one thought of Harmon and Priest as Indian historians.

If you will pardon a personal aside, in January 1946 I went to the University of Wisconsin to study frontier history. To my dismay, I discovered that the university that had produced Frederick Jackson Turner had no frontier historian. Solely because of the time period in which I was interested, I was assigned to the seminar of William B. Hesseltine, a distinguished Civil War and Reconstruction scholar. In the four years I was at Madison, I detected no interest on Hesseltine's part in American Indians—other than his membership in the Loyal Order of Red Men.

I had gone to Wisconsin with an interest in conventional frontier history, not Indian history per se; again, there was no such field of study. But six months after I arrived in Madison, Professor Hesseltine recommended me for a project funded by the state legislature to locate the trail that Black Hawk and his Sac and Fox followers took through Wisconsin in the 1832 war. And Hesseltine would then permit me to expand that research into a dissertation on the Black Hawk War. Needless to say, no one at Madison insisted that I take any anthropology, and my dissertation was a typical one-dimensional version of a frontier conflict, written almost exclusively from the viewpoints of pioneers and government officials.

But I did not have to wait to be educated by New Western History proponents in the error of my ways. The annual meetings and the journal of the American Society for Ethnohistory quickly made me aware of my shortcomings.

Ethnohistory was then a society busy dealing with its own identity crisis. Was ethnohistory a new social science, or simply a branch of anthropology? The relatively few historians in the organization tended to look upon ethnohistory as a method. After the launching of the Western History Association in 1961, some historians who had affiliated with the American Society of Ethnohistory tended to feel more at home in the new organization and joined it, taking their new-found interest in ethnohistory with them.

The debate over the nature of ethnohistory continued. Anthropologists spoke most often on the subject, although a few historians also got in the act. Wilcomb E. Washburn, who had training in history at Harvard although his degree was in American Studies, James C. Olson, then at the University of Nebraska, and Stanley Pargellis of the Newberry Library were historians involved early in the effort to define ethnohistory.[5]

Washburn spoke to the issue in 1960, at a symposium during the annual meeting of what was still called the American Indian Ethnohistoric Conference. He acknowledged that anthropologists were better prepared to do fieldwork, and that historians specialized in research in documentary sources. Nevertheless, he maintained that the two were complementary and both were necessary in the study of Indians. And, Washburn pointed out, two anthropologists—William N. Fenton and John C. Ewers—already had demonstrated that scholars could function effectively both in the field and in the library regardless of their primary training. Washburn went on to propose ethnohistory as a "method of isolating the facts and perceiving them from both sides . . . 'history in the round.'"[6]

Commenting on the papers presented by Washburn and others, anthropologist John Ewers argued for "a combined approach employing as many of the field or library and museum approaches . . . as may be in any way helpful. . . ."[7] In addition to documents, Ewers listed maps, pictures, and artifacts as resources found in libraries and museums, and under field studies he included ethnology, folklore, language, and site exploration.[8]

The object of this multiple attack on the problem was to produce an Indian-centered history based on all the possible sources, to supplement what had been the standard fare—histories of Indian wars and government policy—both too often reflecting the ethnocentricity of the white author. Washburn also proposed new topics to be addressed. In an issue of *Ethnohistory* nearly forty years ago, he suggested several subjects worth exploring.[9] They included statistical studies of the impact of disease on Indians in the Western Hemisphere. By the late 1960s historian Alfred W. Crosby and anthropologist Henry F. Dobyns had begun to address that need. Today even conservative historians accept population estimates of pre-Columbian populations in what is now the United States that are at least four times larger than the estimates used in 1950.

Although historians did not begin to describe their work as ethnohistory until the 1960s, there were those who had broadened their research sufficiently to merit the title. One of the first was Allen W. Trelease, whose *Indian Affairs in Colonial New York*, published in 1960, incorporated ethnological material and made an effort to present an Indian viewpoint.

Robert H. Berkhofer, Jr., whose Ph.D. program had included a minor in anthropology and who thus came more naturally to ethnohistory, was by the mid-1960s exhibiting some of the benefits to be gained from the new approaches. Writing in his *Salvation and the Savage*, published in 1965, of the pre–Civil War efforts to convert Indians to Christianity, Berkhofer sought to demonstrate that both Native Americans and missionaries were behaving "according to their own cultural systems."[10] That same year he published in the spring issue of *Ethnohistory* an essay entitled "Faith and Factionalism among the Senecas: Theory and Ethnohistory."

Ethnohistory would get a boost from another organization that would have a considerable impact on research in the field. This was what is now known as the D'Arcy McNickle Center for the History of the American Indian, at the Newberry Library in Chicago. It opened in 1972, fifteen years before the publication of *Legacy of Conquest*, and by a very rough count has provided research fellowships for at least forty historians at the Center. While it sponsors a variety of seminars and institutes for the nonprofessionals, usually Native Americans, it is through its influence on those holders of its research fellowships that it made an invaluable contribution to the writing of Indian history.

The staff of the Newberry was there not to mentor research in the usual sense, but rather to assist the fellows in exploiting the resources of one of the country's great research libraries. In addition, the Center provided both neophyte and veteran scholars the opportunity on a daily basis to exchange ideas and information in a very stimulating environment.

The contacts with other scholars in the field enabled fellows to become part of a professional network. (I've heard it referred to as the "Newberry Mafia.") From the ranks of the Center's alumni have come the people who today dominate the field of Indian history, and most of them made their mark before the idea of a New Western History had burst on the scene.

The dean of historians associated with the Center is Francis Jennings. With his book published in 1975, *The Invasion of America: Indians, Colonialism, and the Cant of Conquest*, Jennings led the way for a major revision of the history of Indian–white relations in the colonial period. Other historians with Newberry connections who have helped reshape Indian history are James Axtell, R. David Edmunds, Peter Iverson, Frederick E. Hoxie, and Richard White, to mention only a few.

Richard White deserves special mention as the only prominent spokes-man for the New Western History who has done work in Indian history. His prizewinning *The Roots of Dependency: Subsistence, Environment, and Social Change among the Choctaws, Pawnees, and Navajos,* published in 1983, exemplified the interdiscplinary approach that Wilcomb Washburn and others had been calling for in the 1950s.

Having satisfied my historian's urge to put the topic in perspective, it is time to address the content of the New Indian History. I have arbitrarily limited this to a selection of book-length monographs by historians, about Indians in what are now the forty-eight contiguous states, and published since 1987, the year Patricia Limerick's *Legacy of Conquest* launched the New Western History movement. This date is more of a convenience than anything else, if my thesis is correct that the New Indian History was born in the discussions of ethnohistory that flourished in the 1950s and 1960s.

The works to be discussed are in two categories. One contains those fo-cusing on a single tribe or group of tribes, and the other is a catchall category that includes period histories and policy studies. The latter first attracted historians, as the previously cited works of George Dewey Harmon and Loring Benson Priest illustrate. This was to be expected because to shift from schol-arly studies of tariff and farm policies and other facets of government activ-ity to federal Indian policy was not a great leap.

Since 1987 historians have published several monographs that fall into the category of period histories and policy studies. Two by Francis Jennings and Richard White are particularly noteworthy. With *Empire of Fortune* Jennings completed his trilogy that includes *The Invasion of America* and *Ambiguous Iroquois Empire. Empire of Fortune* was designed both as a con-tinuation of his discussion of the covenant chain—his term for the Iroquois–English confederation—and as a counter to the imperialist school of history's version of the Seven Years War. Writing with his customary verve and viv-idness, Jennings gives greater emphasis to the Indian role than did his prede-cessors. Indeed, if he is to be faulted it is because he credits the Iroquois League with a greater degree of unity and influence than it may have en-joyed.

Jennings is happy with the label *ethnohistorian,* as is Richard White. White's *The Middle Ground: Indians, Empires, and Republics in the Great Lakes Region, 1650–1815* makes a conscious effort to place the Indians at the center of the action. Indeed, White declares that he is "practicing 'the new Indian history.'"[11] Moreover, he tries to give Indian women their due for their role in helping establish the middle ground. White, however, is primarily concerned with tribal interaction with the French, British, Americans, and other Indians. Although he is discussing rather familiar topics, he manages to present them in fresh and provocative ways.

White has some interesting things to say about Indian warfare and treatment of captives, and the subject of Indians as warriors continues to attract scholars. Patrick M. Malone's *The Skulking Way of War: Technology and Tactics among the New England Indians* is a brief but valuable study. He credits Indians with adapting quickly to the new technology and considers their employment of firearms to be superior, in some respects, to that of the colonists. It is in his thorough exploitation of museum and private collections of artifacts, as well as the standard library sources, that Malone exemplifies the approach that John Ewers urged.

The Indian wars of the nineteenth century continue to be popular, and at least one book reflects the influence of the New Indian History. Anthony McGinnis's *Counting Coup and Cutting Horses: Intertribal Warfare on the Northern Plains, 1783–1889* is a welcome relief from the oft-told story of warriors versus the cavalry. He concentrates on the fighting *among* the Plains Indians and covers all the major aspects, including motivation, equipment, and tactics.

Missionary work among the Indians is another topic that continues to be popular. William G. McLoughlin, who entered the field of Indian studies through his interest in religious history, was the author of *Champions of the Cherokees: Evan and John B. Jones*. McLoughlin was a prodigious researcher and it is unlikely that we will ever learn more about the Joneses, a father and son who were devoted missionaries to the Cherokees. Over the twenty years that he labored in the field, McLoughlin's work was enriched by a growing concern with Cherokee culture. Toward the end of his career this scholar, who earlier had epitomized traditional scholarship, had begun to think of himself as an ethnohistorian.[12]

Carol Devens leaves no doubt about her alignment with the New Indian History. In *Countering Colonization: Native American Women and Great Lakes Missions, 1630–1900*, she concentrated on the Indian side of the encounter and explains the way in which their reaction to missionary efforts frequently split along gender lines. It was the Indian women who were less susceptible to conversion and who "increasingly identified themselves, and were identified by men, with traditional culture."[13]

Education was another element of government policy. Three books about Indian education that meet the criteria for the New Indian History have been published since 1987. Devon A. Mihesuah and Robert A. Trennert both have written about boarding schools in the late nineteenth and early twentieth centuries, but there the resemblance stops. Mihesuah's *Cultivating the Rosebuds: The Education of Women at the Cherokee Female Seminary, 1881–1909* focuses on a school founded and operated by the Cherokee Nation, a school with a curriculum based on that of what was then called Mount Holyoke Seminary. The Cherokee Female Seminary served as a finishing school for most who attended it, although it also prepared a few Cherokee women for college.

In contrast, Robert Trennert's *The Phoenix Indian School: Forced Acculturation in Arizona, 1891–1935* is more traditional. He deals with a government institution to which students were sent from a variety of tribes and which stressed vocational education. Not surprisingly, Mihesuah found more to admire in the Cherokee seminary than Trennert did in the Phoenix school.

In Trennert's study the voice of the students is muted, as it is in most studies of Indian education. Michael C. Coleman has sought, in his *American Indian Children at School, 1850–1930*, to correct this, assembling reminiscences of a hundred Indian students. The recollections, however, are difficult to evaluate. Conclusions about student life at a particular school seldom can be drawn with confidence from a few reminiscences when hundreds, even thousands, of children passed through the school over a span of several decades.

Acquisition of Indian land, while not usually a stated government objective, was never far from the minds of the members of Congress and of officials of the Indian Service. Two recent studies of this vital topic are Linda S. Parker's *Native American Estate: The Struggle over Indian and Hawaiian Lands*, and Janet A. McDonnell's *Dispossession of the American Indian, 1887–1934*. McDonnell's focus is on what happened between the passage of the Dawes Severalty Act and the decision early in the Indian New Deal to end allotment. Like her mentor, Francis Paul Prucha, she is more evenhanded in assigning blame for the Indian loss of land than some Indian advocates would prefer. McDonnell places "much of the blame" on government personnel, although she also cites Indian resistance to "cultural change" as an explanation for the Native Americans' loss of land between 1887 and 1934.[14]

Linda Parker, by comparing and contrasting the Indian and Hawaiian experiences, attempts something new. She sees obvious parallels between what happened to indigenous peoples at the hands of Americans. In both situations the intruders used the same rationalization for their actions, claiming that private property was a prerequisite for their advancement. And the result was the same, with most of the valuable land ending up in white hands.

There have been several books published recently that relate to Indian natural resources other than land, but only one on that important theme is the work of an historian. This is Robert Doherty's *Disputed Waters: Native Americans and the Great Lakes Fishery*, which examines the efforts of Chippewa and Ottawa bands to secure what they regard as their fishing rights. Personally acquainted with the fishing industry in northern Michigan, Doherty is sympathetic to the Indians' cause. He manages to make sense of an issue that has pitted federal and state agencies against each other and has also divided the Indians.

Historians have been distressingly slow to investigate contemporary Indian problems and issues. An exception is Donald L. Fixico, who published a very useful study in 1986, *Termination and Relocation: Federal Indian Policy, 1945–1960*. Another is Edmund Jefferson Danziger, Jr., whose *Survival and Regeneration: Detroit's American Indian Community* was published in the period under consideration. Traditionally the United States has acknowledged responsibility only for Indians in and near reservations. But Danziger traces the development of a pan-Indian community in Detroit, one that in the previous twenty-five years had gained some recognition and support from the government. Studies of urban Indian populations can give us a new appreciation of Indian cultural persistence and the growth of pan-Indianism.

Turning now to tribal studies, we find them still flourishing. In a few instances, however, tribes also were members of leagues or confederations, the best known of which is the Iroquois. Since the pioneering work of Lewis H. Morgan in the mid-nineteenth century, the Iroquois have had what may be more than their fair share of scholarly attention. As noted earlier, they have been the subjects of the New Indian History as practiced by Francis Jennings. Among others who have worked in Iroquois materials lately, none has done better than Daniel K. Richter. In his *The Ordeal of the Longhouse: The Peoples of the Iroquois League in the Era of European Colonization*, Richter makes excellent use of not only documentary sources but also what archaeologists and anthropologists have discovered about the nature of Iroquois life prior to 1740. In the task he set for himself, presenting "a story of European civilization viewed from the Indian side of the frontier," Richter proved his competence as an ethnohistorian.

Another practitioner of the new school who has made significant contributions to Iroquois history is Laurence M. Hauptman. Since 1987 he has published two volumes that, while very different in scope, are both contributions. Hauptman's *The Iroquois in the Civil War* is conventional narrative history; however, he defined his subject broadly to include both conventional military history and chapters on the home front entitled "Woman at War" and "Children at War." His other recent work is that rare item, a historian's investigation of a state's current Indian policy. *Formulating In-*

dian Policy in New York State takes an acerbic view of the state's political maneuverings at the expense of descendants of New York's original inhabitants. As with Hauptman's other work, it is a fine blend of library and field-work.

If the Iroquois were dominant in the North during the colonial era, the Cherokees and the Creeks were the strongest combinations in the South. Over the years the Cherokees have attracted much scholarly attention, with William McLoughlin being an excellent example. His last work, published posthumously, *After the Trail of Tears: The Cherokee Struggle for Sovereignty, 1839–1880*, revealed the customary exhaustive research we had come to expect from this fine scholar.

Two other historians who have published on the Cherokees in recent years are John R. Finger and Dianna Everett. They are both operating on the periphery of the customary Cherokee studies. Finger's *Cherokee Americans: The Eastern Band of Cherokees in the Twentieth Century* is an authoritative account of the Cherokees who escaped removal. He interviewed extensively to get Cherokee input on their history, as well as thoroughly working the usual library sources. He concluded that in their enclave in the Southeast these Cherokees had succeeded better than their more numerous western kinsmen in preserving their Indianness.

Finger's and Dianna Everett's studies have very little in common. Her's is entitled *The Texas Cherokees: A People between Two Fires, 1819–1840*. She also aspired to write ethnohistory, or at least to 'place the Texas Cherokees in ethnohistorical perspective rather than the perspective of the political history of Texas."[15] The problem she faced was a common one for Indian historians, that of being forced to rely on a record compiled by American and Mexican settlers and officials. Everett could only speculate about the persistence of cultural patterns these outsiders failed to record.

Joel W. Martin, author of *Sacred Revolt: The Muskogees' Struggle for a New World*, also approached his subject in the spirit of the New Indian History. Indeed, he seemed to believe that he was breaking new ground, that previously "historians left those people dead on the battlefield without ever bothering to ask who they were and why they fought."[16] Given earlier work on the Creeks by scholars such as Michael D. Green and J. Leitch Wright, Jr., perhaps Martin overstated his case. He does focus more closely on the Creek religious experience than the historians who have preceded him, although not all scholars will accept the degree to which Martin maintains that the Creeks developed their own "sacred revolt."

One ethnohistorian who places the Creek nativist movement in a larger framework is Gregory Evans Dowd. His *A Spirited Resistance: The North*

American Struggle for Unity, 1745–1815 stresses the intertribal ties among the prophets and the networks they created. He sees "a broadly interconnected movement that produced many visionaries even as it divided communities."[17] Given the tribal orientation of Indians, this is not an easy thesis to maintain. Richard White, in *The Middle Ground,* wrote of common Indian reactions to contact with Europeans in a single region. Dowd attempted something much more ambitious, applying his thesis to the entire area where Indians were reacting to the white intruders. And Dowd saw not only similar patterns of Indian response, but also some evidence of coordinated activity by nativist leaders from a wide range of tribes.

Daniel H. Usner is still another historian who has used the regional approach, although not confining his attention to Indians. The result was an impressive volume, *Indians, Settlers and Slaves in a Frontier Economy: The Lower Mississippi Valley before 1783.* Usner was not trained as an Indian historian. He began as a student of slavery but saw the light, perhaps while a fellow at the Newberry Center. In the course of extensive research he was struck by the interaction of Indians, settlers, and slaves along the lower Mississippi. The result was a study that, while not focused on Indians exclusively, gives us a valuable perspective on the relations among the Choctaws, Chickasaws, and a number of smaller tribes, as well as on their ties with the local settlers and slaves.

Still another exponent of the regional approach is Michael N. McConnell, author of *A Country Between: The Upper Ohio Valley and Its Peoples, 1724–1774.* Unlike Usner, he takes the Indians as his major concern while stressing "the interplay of peoples and interests—Indian, British, and French, economic, political, and cultural."[18] Part of writing New Indian History is to emphasize Indian initiatives, and he does. In McConnell's words: "Ohio Indians continued to face changes and challenges as they had always done: by creatively adapting to new situations, selectively adopting from outsiders, but always acting from within cultural frameworks that provided identity and order in an ever changing—and increasingly unpredictable—world."[19]

Despite the current interest in regional histories, there is still value in the strictly tribal approach as is apparent in a collaborative work by R. David Edmunds and Joseph L. Peyser. Their *The Fox Wars: The Mesquakie Challenge to New France* deals with events in the early eighteenth century. Like most other Indian historians these days, Edmunds and Peyser describe their work as ethnohistory and it is. Exploiting French sources to a greater degree than their predecessors, they also "have tried to incorporate . . . oral traditions and to present these events as much as possible from the Fox perspective."[20] The result is the best explanation yet for the origins of the two-decade-long conflict between the Foxes and the French, fighting that forced the French from the Fox–Wisconsin waterway and far enough east to heighten the tension between France and England and thus help set the stage for the last two colonial wars.

The New Indian History features a growing interest, and appropriately so, in biography. A recent subject was D'Arcy McNickle, long associated with the Newberry Center that now bears his name. Dorothy R. Parker's *Singing an Indian Song: A Biography of D'Arcy McNickle* traces the remarkable career of this mixed-blood Flathead Indian who gained distinction as a novelist, administrator in the Indian Service, and historian/anthropologist. As Parker points out, his affiliation with the Newberry Center, from its inception, was crucial. He helped give it credibility "with both the scholarly and the Indian communities."[21] McNickle operated in the best sense of Indian leadership, constantly seeking consensus when the historians and anthropologists on the advisory board squabbled, and they often did.

This is a good place to stop, although there certainly are other books that might have been discussed. Surely, however, enough has been said to make the case that the New Indian History evolved over the last four decades—antedating the New Western History—and is now firmly in place.

How the ethnohistorical methodology will be employed in the future is a matter about which we can only speculate. Histories of Indian populations of specific regions currently are enjoying some popularity. Nevertheless, Indians continue to identify as tribal members and the states and the federal government so recognize them. Moreover, with all the excitement created by claims of tribal sovereignty over everything from licensing automobiles to the types of gambling in which Indians can engage, the tribal perspective should continue to dominate. As for general histories, Patricia Limerick was correct when she said: "Following federal policy is, in fact, the only route to a clear, chronological, sequential overview of Indian history."[22]

Overall, Indian history is flourishing. We can only hope, however, that scholars will be more inclined to take up where Donald Fixico left off and take on such important developments as repatriation and tribal sovereignty. The issues of today need to be examined—employing the methodology of the New Indian History.

Notes

1. I am indebted to my colleague Donald J. Pisani for a careful reading of this essay in manuscript.

2. Patricia Nelson Limerick, Clyde Milner III, and Charles E. Rankin, eds., *Trails: Toward a New Western History* (Lawrence, Kans., 1991), xi.

3. For the career of the individual with the greatest role in bringing the new organization into being, see Helen Hornbeck Tanner, "Erminie Wheeler-Vogelin (1903–1938), Founder of the American Society for Ethnohistory," *Ethnohistory* 38 (Winter 1991), 58–72. See also Francis Jennings, "A Growing Partnership: Historians, Anthropologists and American History," *Ethnohistory* 29:1 (1982), 21–34.

4. Bruce G. Trigger, "Ethnohistory: Problems and Prospects," *Ethnohistory* 29:1 (1982), 3.

5. James C. Olson, "Some Reflections on Historical Method and Indian History," *Ethnohistory* 5 (Winter 1958), 48–59; Stanley Pargellis, "The Problem of American Indian History," *Ethnohistory* 4 (Spring 1957), 113–24.

6. Wilcomb F. Washburn, "Ethnohistory: 'History in the Round,'" *Ethnohistory* 8 (Winter 1961), 41.

7. John C. Ewers, "Symposium on the Concept of Ethnohistory—Comment," *Ethnohistory* 8 (Summer 1961), 262–70.

8. For a historian's opinion twenty years later, see James Axtell, "Ethnohistory: An Historian's Viewpoint," in Axtell, *The European and the Indian: Essays in the Ethnohistory of Colonial North America* (New York, 1981), 3–16.

9. Wilcomb E. Washburn, "A Moral History of Indian–White Relations: Needs and Opportunities for Study," *Ethnohistory* 4 (Winter 1957), 49.

10. Robert H. Berkhofer, Jr., *Salvation and the Savage: An Analysis of Protestant Missions and American Indian Responses, 1787–1862* (Lexington, Ky., 1965), ix.

11. Richard White, *The Middle Ground: Indians, Empires, and Republics in the Great Lakes Region, 1650–1815* (New York, 1991), xi.

12. William G. McLoughlin, "Rejoinder to Kehoe," *Ethnohistory* 38 (Winter 1991), 74.

13. Carol Devens, *Countering Colonization: Native American Women and Great Lakes Missions, 1630–1900* (Berkeley, 1992), 119.

14. Janet K. McDonnell, *The Dispossession of the American Indian, 1887–1934* (Bloomington, 1991), 124.

15. Dianna Everett, *The Texas Cherokees: A People between Two Fires, 1819–1840* (Norman, 1990), xiv.

16. Joel W. Martin, *Sacred Revolt: The Muskogees' Struggle for a New World* (Boston, 1991), x.

17. Gregory Evans Dowd, *A Spirited Resistance: The North American Struggle for Unity, 1745–1815* (Baltimore, 1992), xix.

18. Michael N. McConnell, *A Country Between: The Upper Ohio Valley and Its Peoples, 1724–1774* (Lincoln, 1992), 4.

19. Ibid., 207.

20. R. David Edmunds and Joseph L. Peyser, *The Fox Wars: The Mesquakie Challenge to New France* (Norman, 1993), xvii.

21. Dorothy R. Parker, *Singing an Indian Song: A Biography of D'Arcy McNickle* (Lincoln, 1922), 240.

22. Patricia Nelson Limerick, *The Legacy of Conquest: The Unbroken Past of the American West* (New York and London, 1987), 195.

3
The Historiography of American Indian and Other Western Women

Glenda Riley

Unlike the introductory chapter here, this essay explores the historiography of women in the American West. Why should a discussion of the writing of western women's history merit such a prominent position in a volume on American Indian history? Simply put, the editor believes that because a significant number of Indians were, and are, female, and that many of them originated in, or still live in, the western United States, it is incumbent upon anyone working in Indian history to understand something about women in the American West, as well as the ways in which the development of western women's history has affected Indian women's history.

What follows indicates that although the writing of western women's history as an organized endeavor is relatively recent, its course is checkered and complex. It also demonstrates that, to its discredit, western women's historiography initially overlooked Indian women. To its credit, however, practitioners gradually recognized and tried to remedy the omission.

Double Jeopardy during the Early Years, to 1984

Traditionally, the history of Indian women suffered double jeopardy. As Professor Hagan has so ably demonstrated, early researchers interested in Indians usually overlooked Native American females. Similarly, those who wrote about western women—long before the feminist movement and the development of social history inspired scholars to retrieve and reinterpret women's stories—also concentrated on Anglo rather than native women.

Consequently, early editors of women's writings brought to light the adventures of such white women as Susan Magoffin, who claimed to be the first Anglo woman in Santa Fe, while only a few revealed the lives of women of color.[1] In addition, in the realm of secondary studies most authors similarly offered to readers various portrayals of Anglo women in the West. In 1879, William Fowler's highly sentimentalized version of women's western experiences, *Woman on the American Frontier*, regaled its readers with descriptions of Anglo "frontier mothers." During the early twentieth century, Emerson Hough similarly portrayed western women as romantic figures in sunbonnets, while Hamlin Garland skimmed over women by simply reinforcing the notion of pioneer mothers. By midcentury, Nancy Ross's *Westward the Women* (1944) and Georgia Read's essay, "Women and Children on the Oregon-California Trail" (also 1944), indicated that women deserved serious study, but most historians continued in the tradition of Frederick Jackson Turner and Walter Prescott Webb by including women in such larger—and highly exclusive—categories as "pioneer" and "settler."[2]

On the one hand, it was fortunate for this rudimentary scholarship of western women that the 1960s witnessed a turning point in both popular and academic attitudes toward women and people of color. Swelling discontent characterized by freedom summers, anti-Vietnam protests, Project Head Start, and emerging feminism brought a rapidly changing awareness of women's and "minority" group issues. In historical circles during the 1960s, western historian T. A. Larson also gave a hint of things to come in an article analyzing woman suffrage in Wyoming.[3] By the early 1970s, with the contemporary feminist movement gaining a voice heard around the world, the pace of scholarship focusing on western women also quickened.[4]

On the other hand, it was less salutary for western women's history during the 1960s and early 1970s that early writers generally followed long-established scholarly custom, taking as their concerns traditional historical questions regarding Anglos' participation in politics and in westward expansion. During these years, even those who identified themselves as historians of western women also adopted as their frameworks customary historical questions and approaches. For example, agricultural historian Mary W. M. Hargreaves broke with tradition and with Walter Prescott Webb's version of Plains history by calling notice to Anglo women on the Great Plains; yet she studied only Anglo women on the Plains. In 1973 Hargreaves wrote about "homesteading and homemaking" on the Plains, and in 1976 she raised queries regarding women's roles in the agricultural settlement of the northern Plains.[5]

By that point, the mid-1970s, women's history—and women graduate students—entered, albeit it in small numbers, academic programs, including those in American and western history. As a result, recently trained female—as well as male—historians took up the cause of adding women to the history of the American West. Although many older practitioners warned of the folly of such a task because women's history lacked adequate sources, these and other determined historians mounted a massive effort to recover women's documents from attics, basements, and uncataloged inclusion in men's archival and manuscript collections.

Within a few years, these researchers helped reshape libraries' and archives' collection policies to include such women's sources as diaries, letters, memoirs, and oral histories, in other words, they let women speak for themselves.[6] These historians also experimented with using such nontraditional resources as family Bibles, marriage registers, wills, police records, legends, and folktales.

As emerging historians of western women defied the establishment, amassed their source materials, and wrote revisionist histories, they aspired to restore women's well-deserved place in western history. Because much of western history focused upon Anglo westward expansion, this restoration necessitated proving and assessing the presence of women in the Anglo westward movement. The first studies were article-length and appeared in a variety of journals ranging from the well-established *Western Historical Quarterly* to the newly founded *Feminist Studies*.[7] Soon book-length studies followed: in 1979, both John Faragher's *Women and Men on the Overland Trail* and Julie Roy Jeffrey's *Frontier Women*.[8]

Despite their innovative focus on women, these historians also followed some of the long-standing approaches they had read and studied for years. Just as western historians emphasized Anglo participants in western expansion—and as early writers on western women had featured Anglo women—so did these writers generally study white women. They especially attempted to destroy such popular stereotypes as the gaunt, overworked frontierswoman, the helpmate, the civilizer, and the "true" woman, replacing them instead with more factual women who participated in everything from running a farm to politics, to the paid labor market.[9]

Granted, historians writing during the late 1960s and 1970s largely overlooked American Indian women. But anyone who lived through those years will remember that historians of western women believed source materials were sparse, knew they could not cope with the languages used in the documents, and saw women of color as a small part of the western population—attitudes that now seem antiquated but constituted real fears at the time. Such historians also struggled mightily against an academic establishment hesitant to allow even white women's topics and courses into the curriculum. This is not intended to excuse what now appears to us to be limited, racist attitudes, but to place these scholars and their work in the context of their own time.

It is also important to add that despite such hindrances—self-imposed and otherwise—researchers were especially quick to recognize *types* of Anglo women, ranging from military women to women religious.[10] Others included an analysis of cross-cultural perspectives, intermarriage, and women of color in their work.[11] More specifically, innovative historians began to consider Native American women and call them to the attention of other scholars. During the mid-1970s, Rayna Green and Beatrice Medicine especially analyzed Native American women in their work.[12] At the same time, others wrote about Latinas. A few scholars, such as Susan Armitage and Lucie Cheng Hirata, undertook the arduous task of reclaiming African-Americans' and Asian-Americans' places in the history of the American West.[13]

Meanwhile, historians of color goaded Anglo historians to expand their horizons further. Throughout the 1970s, at conferences, in book reviews, and in articles, historians of color let their anger seep through or even flare. This proved an effective prod to those who lagged behind in their thinking. At the end of the decade, Joan M. Jensen's and Darlis A. Miller's 1980 essay, "The Gentle Tamers Revisited," reinforced this growing awareness by calling for, among other things, an enlarged incorporation of a multicultural strategy. "We need, above all else," they wrote, "studies firmly based on a comparative multicultural approach to women's history to understand fully the western experience."[14]

During the early 1980s, although some historians continued the critical assault on images and myths,[15] others concentrated on developing and exploring the meaning of multiculturalism. Historians of the early 1980s often had no training in women's history, much less in multicultural studies, but they attempted to respond to criticism. Two book-length studies included ethnic/racial groups of women, while a growing number of articles investigated various types of women.[16]

Yet other scholars of the early 1980s recognized the crucial importance of intergroup relations. Even though they frequently conducted their analysis from an Anglo perspective, they studied perceptions of one group of another, the assimilation process, and intermarriage, friendship, and trade between such types of women as migrants and Indians.[17] This is not the brand of multiculturalism most scholars would advocate today because such treatments of women of color make them seem incidental or secondary, yet for its time it was an important start.

In addition, other researchers devoted their efforts to Native American women, Latinas, African-American women, and Asian women.[18] During the early 1980s, historians of Native American women proved especially vocal. Like other chroniclers of western women, they hoped to restore women to western history, in the process smashing the stock images and stereotypes that had so long shrouded them. Typical titles proclaimed their intent: "The Image of Indian Women," "Reality and Myth," "Resurrecting History's Forgotten Women," and "The Hidden Half."[19] At the same time, a few farsighted scholars even investigated such previously taboo subject areas as lesbianism and cross-gender women among Native Americans.[20]

Besides restoring women to western history, expanding definitions of western peoples, and adding such groups as Native Americans to the story, historians of western women who wrote during the 1970s and early 1980s also hoped to answer burning issues of an intensely feminist era. Did men exploit western women? Were women able to make significant contributions despite a restrictive social system? And if so, what specifically did women achieve?

Researchers disagreed on the extent of women's exploitation, but concurred that western women made numerous "contributions," such as active participation in labor protests, teaching, shaping educational policies, innovating agricultural processes, and "civilizing" the West.[21] Such studies also included a number that recognized the cultural differences of women of color, and assessed their particular accomplishments. For example, one argued that Korean women had moved by virtue of their numerous contributions from men's subordinates to men's partners.[22]

Historians of this period also emphasized individual biographies of women, largely Anglos.[23] White suffragists and such noted Mormon women as Emma Hale Smith proved popular subjects, with emphasis placed on their resistance to the white male system that limited their participation in political or religious life. In addition, a few women of color received attention. A brief biography told African-American Era Bell Thompson's story and established her as one of South Dakota's "daughters."[24]

Finally, some early-period studies tackled such issues as wife abuse and divorce. Given today's supersensitivity to such issues, it is almost impossible to convey a sense of how thoroughly blinded historians were to the underside of family relationships. Despite that, however, during the 1980s such scholars as Melody Graulich and Lillian Schlissel broke the barrier that prevented historians from admitting that supposedly courageous and noble western men sometimes abused and otherwise violated pioneer mothers. Others such as Robert Griswold and Richard Griswold del Castillo indicated that separation, desertion, divorce, and single-parent households existed among both Anglo and Chicano families.[25]

For the most part, this proved to be unwelcome news to perpetrators of the image of a clean, wholesome West based on family values. But because these revelations coincided with Americans' growing awareness of the growth of such social problems as wife and child abuse, desertion, and divorce, western historians winced and admitted that perhaps all was not perfect in the American West.

In evaluating what historians of the early period—prior to the mid-1980s—achieved, it is clear they did indeed attain their first goal, restoring women's place in western history. Early historians also left other important legacies. In the realm of women's contributions, early-period scholars established an enduring belief in women's achievements, which indicated that women not only existed—they mattered. In biography, the initial period clearly identified individual women as role models and achievers. In family studies, they established the desirability and feasibility of studying women in the context of their family structures. Perhaps most importantly, early historians left a strong tradition of an awareness of variations among women, including those of class, race, ethnicity, religion, and occupation.

As a result, American Indian women no longer suffered double jeopardy. By 1984, both historians of women and Indians were aware of the presence and importance of Native American females. The challenge now was incorporating Indian women and their history into the larger picture, as well as becoming increasingly sophisticated in analysis.

The Contemporary Era, Mid-1980s to the Present

In mid-decade, American thinking seemed once more poised on the brink of radical change. In 1984, the Democratic presidential ticket included a woman, Geraldine Ferraro, for the vice presidency. At the same time, national polls indicated that a majority of Americans felt willing to reject traditional gender roles. But radical change failed to materialize. Ferraro lost, while a number of Americans made it clear that they preferred customary ways of thinking.

In western women's scholarship, 1985 seemed a potential crossroads. A number of important books and articles appeared, but it was also a time of reflection about the future.[26] In one historiographical essay, Paula Petrik wrote that perhaps the "gentle tamers" were in transition, about to experience "an altogether different interpretation in the near future." In a similar essay, Elizabeth Jameson concurred by declaring that "western women's history is still on the edge of a great intellectual frontier—not only because of the work that has been done but also because of the promise of new frameworks yet to come."[27]

But much like the American public, scholars rejected revolutionary transformation. Although in 1986 they produced a flurry of scholarship, rather than creating *different* interpretations and *new* frameworks they clearly built upon interpretations already in place. Although post-1985 writers proved innovative, they also drew heavily upon their historiographical heritage.

Most notably, the year 1986 marked a virtual outpouring of work incorporating one of many kinds of multiculturalism. Unsure perhaps of what the term meant and how exactly one practiced multicultural history, contemporary-period historians took the budding awareness of the early years historians and turned it into a virtual mandate for cultural awareness and diversity. In part, scholars expanded the study of such already recognized types of western women as agrarian women, prostitutes, women religious and missionaries, and political activists.[28] But they also added such categories of women as widows and all types of ethnic/racial women to the picture, while at the same time asking increasingly sophisticated questions.[29] In the area of Indian women's history, Paula Gunn Allen especially proved an innovator and a stimulus to further research.[30]

Some of these scholars moving willingly in these directions, while the rage that women of color expressed propelled others. In the process, all grappled with unfamiliar ideas and methods. For one thing, multiculturalism required intensified retrieval of women's documents and oral histories, ranging from those of agrarian women to women of color.[31] Regarding Indian women, this trend resulted in an attempt to capture the traditions, myths, and rituals of, for example, Oglala, Apache, and Lakota women.[32]

Justly, and in harmony with Americans' growing concern with ethnic/racial relations, women of color received the greatest amount of scholarly attention. Of these, Native American women attracted tremendous interest, yet the surface remains barely scratched. Still fighting to destroy tenacious stereotypes and move beyond the "pathology and problems" approach, many historians of Indian women attempt to analyze more complicated issues. Consequently, during the late 1980s and early 1990s historians of Indian women explored such topics as witchcraft, sources of female identity, medical practices and health care, employment and political activities, the impact of women's conservation of traditional culture, and their efforts on behalf of social change.[33]

Two more recent studies of Native American women expanded customary thinking in other ways. In 1993, historian Ted C. Hinckley explored aspects of Tlingit women's history in Alaska, reminding us that the American West includes such noncontiguous areas as Alaska and Hawaii. In the same year, Diana Meyers Bahr followed Los Angeles Indian women from missions to urban areas, thus pointing out that "reservation" and "mission" history tells only part of the Native American's story.[34]

Also exciting and stimulating were developments in the study of Latinas. The year 1987 proved especially rich. In *Cannery Women, Cannery Lives,* Vicki Ruiz analyzed Mexican women and the roles they played in the California food-processing industry during the mid-twentieth century, while Gloria Anzaldúa brought *mestizo* women to notice. Also in 1987, Sarah Deutsch examined intercultural relations between Latinas and Anglos, but concluded that Latinas exercised less power in the urban setting than Ruiz had indicated.[35] Subsequent studies included essays on Mexican pioneer women, women's relation to the law in Spanish New Mexico, and the role of *curanderas* or faith healers.[36]

During the early 1990s, historians of Latinas mounted yet another challenge to historians of women, some of whom had grown complacent with the seeming progress, or at least believed they were moving at a respectable pace. In 1991, Patricia Zavella sharply reminded historians of western women that Latinas came in many varieties and exhibited as much diversity among themselves as any other ethnic/racial group of women.[37] Meanwhile, Antonia Castañeda argued for the necessity of considering not only gender, but race and culture in studying Latinas.[38] Others continued to remonstrate that Chicana stereotypes must be broken.[39]

Such stinging and fully deserved admonishments forced historians of women to widen their scope. Few could continue to view gender as an isolated or all-encompassing category of analysis. Instead, most acknowledged race and ethnicity as important causal factors, which sometimes outweigh gender and at other times intersect with it. Consequently, studies now often take into account at least the intersections of gender, race, and class, and sometimes other variables as well.[40]

But such realizations also led to multiculturalism as a contested space. Was the West favorable for some groups of women, benign for others, and destructive for yet others? Who can best tell a group's story—only a member of that group? These and other related questions vex and often separate historians of western women.

A very different pattern occurred after the mid-1980s in the study of African-American western women. Although African-American women are the most studied group of women of color among historians of U.S. women in general, this is not the case for historians of western women, who largely regard them with an attitude akin to benign neglect.[41] Only a few researchers have undertaken the study of black women in the West, at least in part because of the difficulty in finding source materials (which *are* extant), the existence of fewer numbers of African-Americans than other peoples of color in the West, and a low awareness of such phenomenon as western slavery, black homesteaders, and black female teachers and entrepreneurs.

Among those who have researched black women in the West, several stand out. In 1987, Anne M. Butler's groundbreaking study of black women in western prisons indicated some of the research possibilities. The following year, another historian argued for the significance of western African-American women and listed research opportunities.[42] More recently, in 1993 two essays on black women appeared, one concerning entrepreneur Mary Ellen Pleasant and the other analyzing African-American women in southern California during World War II, with both boding well for the future.[43] After the mid-1980s research concerning Asian-heritage women also blossomed, though perhaps a bit more slowly than most scholars would have liked. Because of language barriers facing non–Asian speaking historians and uncollected source materials concerning Asian women, many historians of Asian women remained in the retrieving and restorative phase. Other studies of Asian American women effectively attacked conventional images that represented Chinese women as prostitutes and Japanese women as geishas, and instead enumerated the contributions of Asian-heritage women.[44] Yet others have looked beyond the boundaries of Asian culture, examining such topics as intercultural marriage.[45]

Contribution history similarly metamorphosed after 1985, turning into an argument for women's agency. The very word *contribution*, which means to give, act, or help bring about, implies that women exercised will, force, or power. Consequently, contemporary-era historians have become more encompassing than simply discussing victimization, exploitation, and cultural dissolution. Even as "new" western historians urge an intensified study of the many ways in which Anglo men mistreated women and peoples of color, historians are pursuing instead an analysis and understanding of the ways in which women exercised agency and resisted "oppression."[46]

In retrospect, it is fairly easy to identify the evolution of contribution history to a belief in agency. As early as 1986, scholars who studied Anglo women incorporated into their titles such telling phrases as "the pace of their own lives," "women's responses to challenges," and "education and change."[47] Following these came such expressions as "progressive spirit," "women's responses to the challenges," "out of the shadows and into the western sun," "equal to the occasion," "sustaining political ambition," and "shaping public policy."[48] Far from being gaunt, overworked, and exploited victims who passively "gave" their skills, labor, and offspring to the development of the West, these women *acted*. They decided what to give, how to give, when to give, and when to withhold their cooperation.[49]

A corresponding proclivity appeared in studies concerning women of color. Gradually, scholars characterized Native American women as responding, speaking out, influencing policy, and utilizing education to implement change.[50] According to one scholar, the Indian woman's awl—usually disregarded as a common female implement—actually symbolized far more than women's labor; it stood for women's power and control as well.[51]

It was historians of women of color who alerted others that exercising agency not only involved overt action, but could entail relatively silent contention as well. Recently, Carol Green Devens effectively demonstrated that women do not need to respond, speak, shape, utilize, or use any other assertive techniques to influence others. Among the Great Lakes Indians analyzed by Devens, women exerted their will and enforced their decisions by resisting and rejecting missionaries' offerings and inducements.[52] These women struggled and resisted in their own way, by picking and choosing, taking what suited them and rejecting what appeared to threaten their position, status, or culture. Their agency was no less forceful for its subtlety.

In the writing of women's biography, contemporary-era historians also have continued and intensified an existing pattern, that of assessing the deeper meanings of women's lives rather than recounting such lives in purely narrative form. In western women's history, individuals have long been important as role models and fodder for surveys, but researchers have increasingly recognized that the study of specific people reveals personal differences that disappear in the data of a survey or a larger study, as well as allowing a scholar to delve into the issue of private motivation. More specifically, although a survey might demonstrate that a certain percentage of women held paid employment, only a biography can explore why a particular woman worked, how she felt about her labor, and what its effects were on her and her family.[53]

Moreover, given the growing interest in western women's agency, interpretive biography can demonstrate how a particular woman exerted her will and influence, why she chose to do so, and what the impact of her action was. As a result of venturing beyond chronological narrative into the realm of interpretation, historians illuminate a woman's achievements and the elements of agency.[54] Thus, peoples' lives, causes, and accomplishments remain a significant form of historical investigation.[55]

Clearly, historians must research greater numbers of women, *and* ask of their lives the larger questions. This can be accomplished by bringing to bear in a new way legends, media, and publicity. Moreover, thanks to several generations of women's historians, including biographers, scholars can place individual western women in the context of American women's history and raise such issues as how did gender shape the subject's life and work, what female values did she accept or reject, how did women's culture affect her work or causes, were her actions feminist in tone and result, why might she have supported or disavowed feminism, why might she have adopted or ignored other causes of the era, what kind of a role model did she provide, and did she dissemble, that is, hide her true feelings and emotions?[56] For western women it is often relevant and revealing to ask additionally how they might have contributed to western mythology and legend.[57]

By the 1990s a growing number of such interpretive biographies appeared. Although all were about Anglo women, they experimented with asking deeper questions about Anglo/Indian relationships. In 1990, for example, Valerie Mathes's study of Helen Hunt Jackson illustrated Jackson's impact and legacy in the arena of the early Indian reform movement. According to Mathes, Jackson influenced both public sentiment and policy through her "formidable writing and research talents." The following year, Julie Roy Jeffrey demonstrated that Narcissa Whitman was willing to marry another missionary to achieve her goal, a mission to Indians living in the Oregon territory. Jeffrey went on to show that although Whitman resisted certain mores of her era to become one of the first Anglo women to cross the Rocky Mountains, she ultimately faced defeat because of other ingrained attitudes. More recently, Shirley Leckie analyzed Elizabeth Custer's decision to deify her deceased husband, General George Armstrong Custer, and carve out a career for herself as a professional widow. Only "a powerful force" could have created the Custer myth, Leckie wrote, and Elizabeth "supplied that force."[58]

Jackson, Whitman, and Custer constitute especially interesting cases. Each wielded will and power to achieve her ends; worked for a cause and created a career for herself in the process; and operated within "acceptable" female boundaries—as a reformer, missionary, and widow—to gain entrance into male-dominated arenas. What is needed, of course, are similar interpretive biographies of women of color. Such Native American women as Sarah Winnemucca, the LaFlesche sisters, Gertrude Bonnin, and Maria Martinez demand interpretive works. Although some argue that the sources are nonexistent, others point out that such women as Martinez can be studied in terms of her pots, her role as a cultural broker, her place in women's history, and her impact on the Pueblo economy.

Historians must also study Native American "subjects" of such women as Jackson, Whitman, and Custer. Here, historian Peggy Pascoe has supplied an important intellectual model. Much as historians of women in general identified and applied the idea of "women's culture" to their research, Pascoe utilized the concept with rich results in relation to western women. In her 1990 study of Protestant women missionaries in the West, Pascoe illustrated how these women used their own values and beliefs to enlarge their influence and increase their power. Pascoe also investigated the intercultural relations in mission homes, aptly cautioning others that "we need to pay less attention to the values at the center of women's culture and more attention to the relationships at its boundaries."[59]

Of course, leaving out the non-Anglo side of the story destroys context, balance, and interaction, and invalidates conclusions. In addition, often the hazy, partial portrayal of non-Anglos is an unjust one of people who appear passive, victimized, and lacking in will. Instead, it would be intriguing indeed to write the stories of such women as Sarah Winnemucca or Maria Martinez and how they interacted with, affected, and converted their Anglo "subjects." Clearly, whether individual or "collective" biography, it must concentrate not just on the feats of the biographies, but on the other side of the story.

At the same time, family studies have also flowered. Contemporary-era family studies illuminate such significant issues as continuities and changes in domestic work roles, expectations of wives and husbands, child-bearing and child-raising patterns, conflicts between women and men, and thousands of other aspects of human inter-relationships.[60] Still, in a 1991 plea for increased attention to the western family, Virginia Scharff poignantly asked "is anybody home on the range?"[61]

Not only did subsequent studies rise to Scharff's challenge by exploring marital and family structures, relationships, and roles, but a few incorporated a multicultural approach by looking across cultures to take into account intermarriage and ethnic/racial family structure.[62] The other side of the coin—divorce—has also proved to be a matter of growing interest during the early 1990s. Rather than continuing to leave it largely to sociologists and counseling psychologists, historians enlarged their work on such topics as the historical development of divorce laws and causal factors of divorce.[63]

Families, of course, also include children, who both deserve and have received more notice. Since the mid-1980s, studies of children have shown that Mormon parents and their children differ markedly from Hispanic families and that Asian families differ from Anglos. Moreover, what parents teach children, how they discipline them, whether they educate them, and whether they hire them out as wageworkers demonstrates a good deal about family structures.[64] During the early 1990s, an allied topic, fertility, also emerged.

This includes research regarding birth control, prenatal care, childbirth, and fertility rates of women in selected areas of the West.[65]

Despite these advances, most family research focuses on Anglo westerners or on one particular group. What is needed are both studies regarding families of color and those that reach across racial and ethnic lines.[66]

Where Is Western Women's History Going?

Where is western women's history headed, for western women in general and for American Indian women in particular?

The obvious place to turn for prophetic glimpses of the future is the self-reflective literature, but historians of western women have seemed somewhat hesitant to contemplate their craft. Although historiographical and review articles appeared before 1985, few authors seemed ready to deal with the thorny issues of theory, philosophy, and deconstruction that were having such great impact on women's history as a whole.[67] Even after 1985, western women's historians did not ponder their output to the extent that women's historians did.[68]

Still, western women's historians have become increasingly involved in such scholarly scrutiny. Because such source materials as diaries often provide western women's historians' stock in trade, a number of researchers have evaluated them and appraised their use as personal autobiography.[69] Historiography and its implications have also taken on greater interest, especially assessments that point out continuities and changes occurring during the past twenty years.[70] Moreover, historiographical essays increasingly show awareness of the importance of a multicultural perspective.[71]

Those who delve into theoretical aspects of writing western women's history also stress the importance of multicultural perspectives, as well as the significance of interdisciplinary studies. They encourage scholars to reach as broadly and widely across culture, class, and race as possible, so as to understand all aspects of women's experiences.[72] Similarly promising and healthy are recent efforts to define and sort out the politics, problems, and possibilities of writing western women's history.[73]

Unfortunately, distrust runs high among historians of western women, a distrust that demands resolution through cooperation and communication. One cause for suspicion is that the logical outcome of the recent recognition of intersections of race, class, and gender also suggests that such specialties as women's, Indian, Latino, African-American, and Asian-American history overlap. Practitioners therefore must consider more fully and resolve the

Balkanization of Women's, Gender, Native American, Latino, African-American, Asian Studies research, perspectives, and programs. Who will win and who will lose?

Another underlying factor of dissension is the need for scholars to question the ideological wisdom of continuing to pursue separate categories of study and research. Do historians really want to perpetuate socially constructed groupings as ethnicity and race in the thinking of students, scholars, and thus future generations? Or would they rather seek out and develop alternatives?

Looking back, we can see that in the United States both laypeople and scholars have experienced thus far three stages in the evolution of their attitudes toward specific groups of people. During the first, one group of people often disparaged and looked down on others. Race, ethnicity, gender, religion, age, and a host of other characteristics were reasons enough to dislike others, criticize them, and treat them in a discriminatory manner. During the second phase, however, people "discovered" the rich history, culture, and contributions of formerly disparaged groups. People actively sought out diversity, discovered and explored differences among types of people, valued such dissimilarities, and attempted to strengthen intergroup relationships.

In stage three, which we now face, people struggle with—or against—the issues inevitability raised by stage two: How can diversity, affirmative action, and fairness be incorporated into American society? In academia, a similar conflict rages. A growing number of scholars—both of color and Anglo—give academic voice to previously dismissed groups of people. In so doing, it is impossible to overlook the exploitation, victimization, colonization, and other ills that occurred in the past. Bitterness exists, but so does a search for fairly understanding and evaluating all groups of people.

This creates an unprecedented opportunity to pioneer a fourth level, one that searches instead for similarities among groups and identifies the qualities that unify whites and blacks, men and women, Anglos and Indians, English and Spanish speakers, and other categories of people as human beings, as Americans, and as westerners. Such a revolution would not only affect academia, but might also help resolve some of the segmentation of societies occurring across the world today.

Of course, this will involve effort and sacrifice. Historians will have to overcome language barriers, lack of cultural awareness, and suspicion of scholars different from themselves. Also, replacing a linear approach that analyzes events and institutions group by group with a pluralistic perspective that studies events and institutions in themselves *and* includes all groups could very well reshape historical insights.

Historians of western women must also address the implications of assigning agency to women. Two recent studies, which have probed the impact of native women leaders in Alaska and Hawaii, have reevaluated women's political efforts.[74] As a consequence of the growing emphasis on women's agency, a new definition of power is emerging: one can exercise power not only through action, but also by refusing to accept or cooperate. This interpretation could restructure historians' conceptions and their study of power relationships between, for example, politicians and their constituents, employers and employees, and especially men and women.

This development demonstrates deconstruction at its exciting and limitless best, but it also poses some dangers. For instance, most "agency" studies imply that women's ability to preserve existing gender system was beneficial to them. The more individual women such as Libby Custer used gender expectations to get what they wanted, or women of a particular group were able to maintain their customary roles, the more scholars have imputed influence to them. But was it helpful for Custer and others to cling to what were often unequal gender patterns? Would it perhaps prove enlightening to at least explore women's resistance as a conservative tendency that trapped them in old ways?

In addition, scholars have left unanswered the relationship between motives and agency. Did resistant women realize they wielded a form of power? According to Devens, Great Lakes Indian women "may well have been responding to the redefinition of female and male identities and status."[75] But it is as likely that they acted on the basis of their prescribed gender roles to conserve their cultures and protect their heritages for their children, or even out of a human need to exercise a certain amount of control over their own lives.

This raises other related questions. If women acted unconsciously, did their actions demonstrate agency or was agency simply coincidental? How meaningful was the ability to influence others if a woman did not recognize her ability or wield it to achieve certain ends? If a woman had no conscious awareness of her power was it truly power?

Moreover, does imputing power to certain individuals distort history? Do we reshape women's lives to suit our own attitudes regarding women?[76] Historian Richard White has charged that some historians tend "to reify culture and to see it as a shield magically holding back" exploitation and oppression.[77] Clearly, scholarly zeal to demonstrate that women were willful and resistive must not wipe injustices from the historical record.

Overall, for American Indian women's history the evolution of western women's history into such complex and sophisticated patterns is more positive than negative. Historians of western women have helped—albeit grudgingly at times—open the way for extensive study and growing appreciation of Indian women's history. They have developed diverse methodologies and theories that offer tremendous implications for increased understanding of Indian women's history. And western women's history promises much more for the future. It is an enterprise charged with the potential to rewrite not only western women's history, but also the history of Native Americans and, thus, of the West itself.

Notes

The author would like to express her appreciation to Susan H. Armitage of Washington State University and Anne M. Butler of Utah State University for their insights, suggestions, and collegiality during the preparation of this paper.

1. Susan S. Magoffin, *Down the Santa Fe Trail and into Mexico: The Diary of the Susan Shelby Magoffin, 1846–47* (New Haven, 1926); Teresa Vielé, *"Following the Drum": A Glimpse of Frontier Life* (New York, 1858); and Era Bell Thompson, *American Daughter* (Chicago, 1946). For other examples, see Virginia Reed Murphy, "Across the Plains in the Donner Party, 1846," *Century Magazine* 42 (July 1891), 409–26; Frances M. A. Roe, *Army Letters from an Officer's Wife, 1871–1888* (New York, 1909); Lavinia H. Porter, *By Ox Team to California* (Oakland, Calif., 1910); Sarah Royce, *A Frontier Lady* (New Haven, 1932); Raymond S. Brandes, "Times Gone by in Alta California: Recollections of Señora Doña Juana Machado Alipáz de Ridington," *Historical Society of South California Quarterly* 41 (September 1959), 195–240; and Elinore Pruitt Stewart, *Letters of a Woman Homesteader* (Lincoln, 1961).

2. William W. Fowler, *Woman on the American Frontier* (1879; repr., New York, 1970); Emerson Hough, *The Passing of the Frontier* (New Haven, 1921); Hamlin Garland, *A Pioneer Mother* (Chicago, 1922); Nancy Wilson Ross, *Westward the Women* (New York, 1944); Georgia Willis Read, "Women and Children on the Oregon–California Trail in the Gold-Rush Years," *Missouri Historical Review* 34 (October 1944), 1–23. For other early interpretations, see Everett Dick, *The Sod-House Frontier, 1845–1870* (New York, 1937), and "Sunbonnet and Calico, The Homesteader's Consort," *Nebraska History* 47 (March 1966), 3–13; Ruth Tressman, "Home on the Range," *New Mexico Historical Review* 26 (January 1951), 1–17; and Helena H. Smith, "Pioneers in Petticoats," *American Heritage* 10 (February 1959), 36–39, 101–3.

3. T. A. Larson, "Woman Suffrage in Wyoming," *Pacific Northwest Quarterly* 56 (April 1965), 57–66. See also T. A. Larson, "Dolls, Vassals, and Drudges—Pioneer Women in the West," *Western Historical Quarterly* 3 (January 1972), 5–16; Larson, "The Women's Rights Movement in Idaho," *Idaho Yesterdays* 16 (Spring 1972), 2–15, 18–19; Larson, "Women's Role in the West," *Montana, The Magazine of West-*

ern History 24 (Summer 1974), 2–11; Larson, "Home Rule on the Range," in Daniel Tyler, ed., *Western American History in the Seventies* (Fort Collins, Colo., 1973); Larson, "The Woman Suffrage Movement in Washington," *Pacific Northwest Quarterly* 67 (April 1976), 9–62; and Larson, "Wyoming's Contribution to the Regional and National Women's Rights Movement," *Annals of Wyoming* 52 (Spring 1980), 2–14.

4. See, for example, Robert L. Munkres, "Wives, Mothers, Daughters: Women's Life on the Road West," *Annals of Wyoming* 42 (October 1970), 191–224. In addition, a few popular accounts appeared during these years, such as Beverly Larsen, *The Brave Ones: Early Iowa Pioneer Women* (n.p., 1971).

5. Mary W. M. Hargreaves, "Homesteading and Homemaking on the Plains: A Review," *Agricultural History* 47 (April 1973), 156–63, and "Women in the Agricultural Settlement of the Northern Plains," *Agricultural History* 50 (January 1976), 179–89.

6. See, for example, Joseph Snell, ed., "Roughing It on Her Kansas Claim: The Diary of Abbie Bright, 1870–1871," *Kansas Historical Quarterly* 37 (Autumn 1971), 233–68, and (Winter 1971), 394–428; Frank B. Linderman, *Pretty-Shield: Medicine Woman of the Crows* (Lincoln, 1972); Christiane Fischer, ed., *Let Them Speak for Themselves: Women in the American West, 1849–1900* (Hamden, Conn., 1977); Lillian Schlissel, "Women's Diaries on the Western Frontier," *American Studies* 18 (Spring 1977), 87–100, and *Women's Diaries of the Westward Journey* (New York, 1982); Elizabeth Hampsten, *Read This Only to Yourself: The Private Writings of Midwestern Women, 1880–1910* (Bloomington, 1982); Susan H. Armitage, "Reluctant Pioneers," in Helen W. Stauffer and Susan J. Rosowki, eds., *Women and Western American Literature* (Troy, N.Y., 1982), 40–51; Patricia Preciado Martin, *Images and Conversations: Mexican Americans Recall a Southwestern Past* (Tucson, 1983); and Rayna Green, ed., *That's What She Said: Contemporary Poetry and Fiction by Native American Women* (Bloomington, 1984).

7. Christine Stansell and Johnny Faragher, "Women and Their Families on the Overland Trail to California and Oregon, 1842–1867," *Feminist Studies* 2 (1975), 150–55; Glenda Riley, "Women Pioneers in Iowa," *The Palimpsest* 57 (March/April 1976), 34–53, and "Images of the Frontierswoman: Iowa as a Case Study," *Western Historical Quarterly* 8 (April 1977), 189–202; and Lillian Schlissel, "Mothers and Daughters on the Western Frontier," *Frontiers* 3 (Fall 1979), 29–33.

8. John Mack Faragher, *Women and Men on the Overland Trail* (New Haven, 1979); and Julie Roy Jeffrey, *Frontier Women: The Trans-Mississippi West, 1840–1880* (New York, 1979).

9. Examples are Beverly J. Stoeltje, "'A Helpmate for Man Indeed': The Image of the Frontier Woman," *Journal of American Folklore* 88 (January-March 1975), 25–41; Sheryll Patterson-Black, "Women Homesteaders on the Great Plains Frontier," *Frontiers* 1 (Spring 1976), 67–88; and Riley, "Images of the Frontierswoman."

10. See Patricia Stallard, *Glittering Misery: Dependents of the Indian Fighting Army* (San Rafael, Calif., 1978); and Susan C. Peterson, "From Paradise to Prairie: The Presentation Sisters in Dakota, 1880–1896," *South Dakota History* 10 (Summer 1980), 210–22.

11. Beverly Trulio, "Anglo-American Attitudes toward New Mexican Women," *Journal of the West* 12 (April 1973), 229–39; Jane Dysart, "Mexican Women in San Antonio, 1830–1860: The Assimilation Process," *Western Historical Quarterly* 7 (October 1976), 365–75; Joan M. Jensen, "Women Teachers, Class and Ethnicity," *Southwest Economy and Society* 4 (Winter 1978–1979), 3–13; and Nancy C. Benson, "Pioneering Women of New Mexico," *El Palacio* 85 (1979), 8–13, 34–38.

12. Rayna Green, "The Pocahontas Perplex: The Image of Indian Women in American Culture," *Massachusetts Review* 16 (Autumn 1975), 698–714; and Beatrice Medicine, "Bibliography of Native American Women," *Indian Historian* 8 (Summer 1975), 51–53. See also Mary E. Fleming Mathur, "Who Cares . . . that a Woman's Work Is Never Done?" *Indian Historian* 4 (Summer 1971), 11–16.

13. For Latinas, see Rosaura Sánchez and Rosa Martinez Cruz, eds., *Essays on La Mujer* (Los Angeles, 1977); Roxanne Dunbar, "Colonialism and the Role of Women: The Pueblos of New Mexico," *Southwest Economy and Society* 4 (Winter 1978–1979), 28–46; and Alfredo Mirandé and Evangelina Enríquez, *La Chicana: The Mexican-American Woman* (Chicago, 1979). For African-American women, see Sue Armitage, Theresa Banfield, and Sarah Jacobus, "Black Women and Their Communities in Colorado," *Frontiers* 2 (Spring 1977), 45–51; Lawrence B. DeGraaf, "Race, Sex, and Region: Black Women in the American West, 1850–1920," *Pacific Historical Review* 49 (May 1980), 285–314; and Lynda F. Dickson, "The Early Club Movement among Black Women in Denver: 1890–1925" (Ph.D. diss., University of Colorado, Boulder, 1982). For Asian women, see Lucie Cheng Hirata, "Free, Indentured, Enslaved: Chinese Prostitutes in Nineteenth-century America," *Signs* 5 (Autumn 1979), 3–29; and Yuji Ichioka, "*Amerika Nadeshiko*: Japanese Immigrant Women in the United States, 1900–1924," *Pacific Historical Review* 49 (May 1980), 339–58.

14. Joan M. Jensen and Darlis A. Miller, "The Gentle Tamers Revisited: New Approaches to the History of Women in the American West," *Pacific Historical Review* 49 (May 1980), 213.

15. Those concerned with images during the early 1980s include Susan H. Armitage, "Western Women: Beginning to Come into Focus," *Montana, The Magazine of Western History* 32 (Summer 1982), 2–9, and "Women and Men in Western History: A Stereotypical Vision," *Western Historical Quarterly* 16 (October 1985), 380–95; Elizabeth Jameson, "Women as Workers, Women as Civilizers: True Womanhood in the American West," *Frontiers* 7 (1984), 1–8; and June O. Underwood, "Western Women and True Womanhood: Culture and Symbol in History and Literature," *Great Plains Quarterly* 5 (Spring 1985), 93–106.

16. Glenda Riley, *Frontierswomen: The Iowa Experience* (Ames, 1981; 2d ed., 1994); and Sandra L. Myres, *Westering Women and the Frontier Experience* (Albuquerque, 1983). Regarding prostitutes, see Anne M. Butler, "Military Myopia: Prostitution on the Frontier," *Prologue* 13 (Winter 1981), 233–50; Paula Petrik, "Prostitution in Helena, Montana, 1865–1900," *Montana, The Magazine of Western History* 31 (Spring 1981), 28–41, and "Strange Bedfellows: Prostitution, Politicians and Moral Reform in Helena, Montana, 1885–1887," *Montana, The Magazine of Western History* 35 (Summer 1985), 2–13; and Mary Murphy, "The Private Lives

of Public Women: Prostitution in Butte, Montana, 1878–1917," *Frontiers* 7 (Fall 1984), 30–35. For military women, see Darlis A. Miller, "Foragers, Army Women, and Prostitutes," in Joan M. Jensen and Darlis A. Miller, eds., *New Mexico Women: Intercultural Perspectives* (Albuquerque, 1986). For women Religious, see Susan C. Peterson, "Religious Communities of Women in the West: The Presentation Sisters' Adaptation to the Northern Plains Frontier," *Journal of the West* 21 (April 1982), 65–70, and "Doing 'Women's Work': The Grey Nuns at Fort Totten Indian Reservation, 1874–1900," *North Dakota History* 52 (Spring 1985), 18–25. For Mormon women, see Maureen Ursenbach Beecher, "Women's Work on the Mormon Frontier," *Utah Historical Quarterly* 49 (Summer 1981), 276–90; Jessie L. Embry, "Effects of Polygamy on Mormon Women," *Frontiers* 7 (Fall 1984), 56–61; Jessie L. Embry and Martha S. Bradley, "Mothers and Daughters in Polygamy," *Dialogue* 18 (Fall 1985), 99–107; and D. Gene Pace, "Wives of Nineteenth-Century Mormon Bishops: A Quantitative Analysis," *Journal of the West* 22 (April 1982), 49–57.

17. See Darlis A. Miller, "Cross-Cultural Marriages in the Southwest: The New Mexico Experience, 1846–1900," *New Mexico Historical Review* 57 (October 1982), 335–60; Sandra L. Myres, "Mexican Americans and Westering Anglos: A Feminine Perspective," *New Mexico Historical Review* 57 (October 1982), 317–33; and Glenda Riley, *Women and Indians on the Frontier, 1820–1915* (Albuquerque, 1984).

18. Examples are, Janet Lecompte, "The Independent Women of Hispanic New Mexico, 1821–1846," *Western Historical Quarterly* 12 (January 1981), 17–35; and Harold E. Hinds and Charles Tatum, "Images of Women in Mexican Comic Books," *Journal of Popular Culture* 18 (Summer 1984), 146–62. See also Alma García, "The Development of Chicana Feminist Discourse, 1970–1980," *Gender and Society* 3 (1989), 217–38. See, for example, Nobuya Tsuchida, ed., *Asian and Pacific American Experiences: Women's Perspectives* (Minneapolis, 1982); Reva Clar and William M. Kramer, "Chinese–Jewish Relations in the Far West: 1850–1950," *Western States Jewish Historical Quarterly* 15 (January 1983), 132–53; Asian American Studies Center of the University of California, Los Angeles, and the Chinese Historical Society of South California, *Linking Our Lives: Chinese American Women of Los Angeles* (Los Angeles, 1984); and Sucheng Chan, "Chinese Livelihood in Rural California: The Impact of Economic Change, 1860–1880," *Pacific Historical Review* 53 (August 1984), 273–307.

19. Maryann Oshana, "Native American Women in Westerns: Reality and Myth," *Frontiers* 6 (Fall 1981), 46–50; Rosemary and Joseph Agonito, "Resurrecting History's Forgotten Women: A Case Study from the Cheyenne Indians," *Frontiers* 6 (Fall 1981), 8–16; Patricia Albers and Beatrice Medicine, eds., *The Hidden Half: Studies of Plains Indian Women* (Washington, D.C., 1983). See also Rayna Green, "Native American Women," *Signs* 6 (Winter 1980), 218–67; Margot Liberty, "Hell Came with Horses: Plains Indian Women in the Equestrian Era," *Montana, The Magazine of Western History* 32 (Summer 1982), 10–19; Glenda Riley, "Some European (Mis) Perceptions of American Indian Women," *New Mexico Historical Review* 59 (July 1984), 237–66; and Gretchen M. Bataille and Kathleen Mullen Sands, *American Indian Women: Telling Their Lives* (Lincoln,, 1984).

20. See, for example, Evelyn Blackwood, "Sexuality and Gender in Certain Na-

tive American Tribes: The Case of Cross-Gender Females," *Signs* 10 (Autumn 1984), 27–42.

21. For those discussing exploitation, see Christine Stansell, "Women on the Great Plains, 1865–1890," *Women's Studies* 4 (1976), 87–98; June Sochen, "Frontier Women: A Model for All Women?" *South Dakota History* 7 (Winter 1976), 35–56; Lillian Schlissel, "Diaries of Frontier Women: On Learning to Read the Obscured Patterns," in Mary Kelley, ed., *Woman's Being, Woman's Place: Female Identity and Vocation in American History* (Boston, 1979), 55–66; Jeannie McKnight, "American Dream, Nightmare Underside: Diaries, Letters, and Fiction of Women on the American Frontier," in L. L. Lee and Merrill Lewis, eds., *Women, Women Writers, and the West* (Troy, N.Y., 1979), 25–43; and John Mack Faragher, "History from the Inside-Out: Writing the History of Women in Rural America," *American Quarterly* 33 (Winter 1981), 537–57. For those stressing contributions, see Carlos A. Schwantes, "Western Women in Coxey's Army in 1894," *Arizona and the West* 26 (Spring 1984), 5–20; Harriette Andreadis, "A Woman's Commonwealth: A Study in the Coalescence of Social Forms," *Frontiers* 7 (Summer 1984), 79–86; Polly Welts Kaufman, *Women Teachers on the Frontier* (New Haven, 1984); Katherine Harris, "Sex Roles and Work Patterns among Homesteading Families in Northeastern Colorado, 1873–1920," *Frontiers* 7 (Summer 1984), 43–49; and June O. Underwood, "Civilizing Kansas: Women's Organizations, 1880–1920," *Kansas History* 7 (Winter 1984–85), 291–306.

22. Among those who assessed the contributions of women of color are Mario T. García, "The Chicana in American History: The Mexican Women of El Paso, 1880–1920: A Case Study," *Pacific Historical Review* 49 (May 1980), 315–38; Valerie S. Mathes, "A New Look at the Role of Women in Indian Society," *American Indian Quarterly* 2 (Summer 1975), 131–39, and "Native American Women in Medicine and the Military," *Journal of the West* 21 (April 1982), 41–48; Priscilla K. Buffalohead, "Farmers, Warriors, Traders: A Fresh Look at Ojibway Women," *Minnesota History* 48 (Summer 1983), 236–44; Ann Patton Malone, *Women on the Texas Frontier: A Cross-Cultural Perspective*, Southwestern Studies Monograph No. 70 (El Paso, 1983); and Susan L. Johnson, "Sharing Bed and Board: Cohabitation and Cultural Differences in Central Arizona Mining Towns," *Frontiers* 7 (Fall 1984), 36–42. The argument regarding Korean women is made in Eun Sik Yang, "Korean Women of America: From Subordination to Partnership, 1903–1930," *Amerasia* 11 (1984), 1–28.

23. See, for example Elizabeth C. MacPhail, "Lydia Knapp Horton: A 'Liberated' Woman in Early San Diego," *Journal of San Diego History* 27 (Winter 1981), 17–41; and Patricia V. Horner, "Mary Richardson Walker: The Shattered Dreams of a Missionary Woman," *Montana, The Magazine of Western History* 32 (Summer 1982), 20–31.

24. Examples are Linda Thatcher, ed., "'I Care Nothing for Politics': Ruth May Fox, Forgotten Suffragist," *Utah Historical Quarterly* 49 (Summer 1981), 239–53; Linda King Newell and Valeen Tippets Avery, *Mormon Enigma: Emma Hale Smith: Prophet's Wife, 'Elect Lady,' Polygamy's Foe, 1804–1879* (Garden City, N.Y., 1984); and Kathie Ryckman Anderson, "Era Bell Thompson: A North Dakota Daughter," *North Dakota History* 49 (Fall 1982), 11–18.

25. Melody Graulich, "Violence against Women in Literature of the Western

Family," *Frontiers* 7 (Summer 1984), 14–20; Robert L. Griswold, "Apart but Not Adrift: Wives, Divorce, and Independence in California, 1850–1890," *Pacific Historical Review* 49 (May 1980), 265–84, and *Family and Divorce in California, 1850–1890* (Albany, N.Y., 1982). See also Lillian Schlissel, "Frontier Families: Crisis in Ideology," in Sam B. Girgus, ed., *The American Self: Myth, Ideology, and Popular Culture* (Albuquerque, 1981), 155–65; and Richard Griswold del Castillo, *La Familia: Chicano Families in the Urban Southwest, 1848 to the Present* (Notre Dame, 1984).

26. Articles include Patricia Zavella, "'Abnormal Intimacy': The Varying Work Networks of Chicana Cannery Workers," *Feminist Studies* 11 (Fall 1985), 542–57; Linda Peavy and Ursula Smith, "Women in Waiting in the Westward Movement: Pamela Dillin Fergus and Emma Stratton Christie," *Montana, The Magazine of Western History* 35 (Spring 1985), 2–17; and Petrik, "Strange Bedfellows." For an important book, see Anne M. Butler, *Daughters of Joy, Sisters of Misery* (Urbana, 1985).

27. Paula Petrik, "The Gentle Tamers in Transition: Women in the Trans-Mississippi West," *Feminist Studies* 11 (Fall 1985), 682; and Elizabeth Jameson, "Toward a Multicultural History of Women in the Western United States," *Signs* 13 (1988), 791.

28. For agrarian women, see, for example, Deborah Fink, *Open Country, Iowa: Rural Women, Tradition and Change* (Albany, N.Y., 1986), and *Agrarian Women: Wives and Mothers in Rural Nebraska, 1880–1940* (Chapel Hill, 1992); Joan M. Jensen, "'I've Worked, I'm Not Afraid of Work': Farm Women in New Mexico, 1920–1940," *New Mexico Historical Review* 61 (January 1986), 27–52; Ann Webb, "Forgotten Persephones: Women Farmers on the Frontier," *Minnesota History* 50 (Winter 1986), 134–48; and Marilyn Irvin Holt, "Farm Women, Domestic Economy, and South Dakota's Agrarian Press," *South Dakota History* 24 (Summer 1994), 77–98. For missionaries, see Ruth Ann Alexander, "Gentle Evangelists: Women in Dakota Episcopal Missions, 1867–1900," *South Dakota History* 24 (Winter 1994), 174–93. For political activists, see Michael E. Goldberg, "Non-Partisan and All-Partisan: Rethinking Woman Suffrage and Party Politics in Gilded Age Kansas," *Western Historical Quarterly* 25 (Spring 1994), 21–44. For prostitutes, see Butler, *Daughters of Joy, Sisters of Misery*; and for women Religious, see Susan Peterson and Courtney Vaughn-Roberson, *Women with Vision: The Presentation Sisters of South Dakota, 1880–1985* (Urbana, 1988).

29. For widows, see Arlene Scadron, ed., *On Their Own: Widows and Widowhood in the American Southwest, 1848–1939* (Urbana, 1988). For ethnic/racial women, see, for example, Marilyn Dell Brady, "Kansas Federation of Colored Women's Clubs, 1900–1930," *Kansas History* 9 (Spring 1986): 19–31; H. Elaine Lindgren, "Ethnic Women Homesteading on the Plains of North Dakota," *Great Plains Quarterly* 9 (Summer 1989), 157–73; Linda Schelbitzki Pickle, "Rural German-Speaking Women in Early Nebraska and Kansas: Ethnicity as a Factor in Frontier Adaptation," *Great Plains Quarterly* 9 (Fall 1989), 239–51; and Isabel Kaprielian-Churchill, "Armenian Refugee Women: The Picture Brides, 1920–1930," *Journal of American Ethnic History* 12 (Spring 1993), 3–29. See also Jameson, "Toward a Multicultural History of

Women in the Western United States," 761–91.

30. Paula Gunn Allen, *The Sacred Hoop: Recovering the Feminine in American Indian Tradition* (Boston, 1986).

31. For agrarian women, see Carol Fairbanks and Bergine Hakenson, eds., *Writings of Farm Women, 1840–1940: An Anthology* (New York, 1990); and Ruth B. Moynihan, Susan Armitage, and Christiane Fischer Dichamp, eds., *So Much to Be Done: Women Settlers on the Mining and Ranching Frontier* (Lincoln, 1990). For Latinas, see Edith Powers, trans., *Singing for My Echo: Memories of Gregorita Rodriguez, A Native Healer of Santa Fe* (Santa Fe, 1987); Tey Diana Rebolledo, Erlinda Gonzales-Berry, and Teresa Márquez, eds., *Las Muyeres Hablan: An Anthology of Nuevo Mexicana Writers* (Albuquerque, 1988); Gloria Ricci Lothrop, ed., "Introducing Seven Women of the Hispanic Frontier: A Series," *The Californians* 8 (May/June 1990), 14; and Patricia Preciado Martin, *Songs My Mother Sang to Me: An Oral History of Mexican American Women* (Tucson, 1992). For Asian women, see Shirley Geok-Lin Lim, Mayumi Tsutakawa, and Margarita Donnelly, eds., *The Forbidden Stitch: An Asian American Women's Anthology* (Corvallis, Ore., 1989). For African-American women, see Thompson, *American Daughter*.

32. Marla M. Powers, *Oglala Women: Myth, Ritual, and Reality* (Chicago, 1986); H. Henrietta Stockel, *Women of the Apache Nation: Voices of Truth* (Reno, 1991); and Mark St. Pierre, trans., *Madonna Swan: A Lakota Woman's Story* (Norman, 1991). See also C. J. Brafford and Laine Thom, comps., *Dancing Colors: Paths of Native American Women* (San Francisco, 1992).

33. Jodye Lynn Dickson, "Amazons, Witches and 'Country Wives': Plains Indian Women in Historical Perspective," *Annals of Wyoming* 59 (Spring 1987), 48–56; Rebecca Tsosie, "Changing Women: The Cross-Currents of American Indian Feminine Identity," *American Indian Culture and Research Journal* 12 (1988), 1–37; Devon I. Abbott, "Medicine for the Rosebuds: Health Care at the Cherokee Female Seminary, 1876–1909," *American Indian Culture and Research Journal* 12 (1988), 59–71; Theda Perdue, "Cherokee Women and the Trail of Tears," *Journal of Women's History* 1 (Spring 1989), 14–30; Lisa E. Emmerich, "'Right in the Midst of My Own People': Native American Women and the Field Matron Program," *American Indian Quarterly* 15 (Spring 1991), 201–16; and Gail H. Landsman, "The 'Other' as Political Symbol: Images of Indians in the Woman Suffrage Movement," *Ethnohistory* 39 (Summer 1992), 247–84.

34. Ted C. Hinckley, "Glimpses of Societal Change among Nineteenth-Century Tlingit Women," *Journal of the West* 32 (July 1993), 12–24; and Diana Meyers Bahr, *From Mission to Metropolis: Cupeno Indian Women in Los Angeles* (Norman, 1993).

35. Vicki L. Ruiz, *Cannery Women, Cannery Lives: Mexican Women, Unionization, and the California Food Processing Industry, 1930–1950* (Albuquerque, 1987); Gloria Anzaldúa, *Borderlands/La Frontera: The New Mestiza* (San Francisco, 1987); and Sarah Deutsch, "Women and Intercultural Relations: The Case of Hispanic New Mexico and Colorado," *Signs* 12 (Summer 1987), 719–39, and *No Separate Refuge: Culture, Class, and Gender on an Anglo-Hispanic Frontier in the American Southwest, 1880–1940* (New York, 1987).

36. Frances R. Conley, "Martina Didn't Have a Covered Wagon: A Speculative

Reconstruction," *The Californians* 7 (March-August 1989), 48–54; Rosalind Z. Rock, "'*Pido y Suplico*': Women and the Law in Spanish New Mexico, 1697–1763," *New Mexico Historical Review* 65 (April 1990), 145–59; and Bobette Perrone, H. Henrietta Stockle, and Victoria Krueger, *Medicine Women, Curanderas, and Women Doctors* (Norman, 1989).

37. Patricia Zavella, "Reflections on Diversity among Chicanas," *Frontiers* 12 (Spring 1991), 75.

38. Antonia I. Castañeda, "Gender, Race, and Culture: Spanish-Mexican Women in the Historiography of Frontier California," *Frontiers* 11 (Winter 1990), 8–20, and "Women of Color and the Rewriting of Western History: The Discourse, Politics, and Decolonization of History," *Pacific Historical Review* 61 (November 1992), 501–34.

39. Betty LaDuke, "Yolanda Lopez: Breaking Chicana Stereotypes," *Feminist Studies* 20 (Spring 1994), 117–30.

40. Rosaura Sánchez, "The History of Chicanas: A Proposal for a Materialist Perspective," in Adelaida R. del Castillo, ed., *Between Borders: Essays on Mexicana/Chicana History* (Encino, Calif., 1990), 1–30; National Association for Chicano Studies, *Chicana Voices: Intersections of Class, Race, and Gender* (Albuquerque, 1990); Devon A. Mihesuah, "Too Dark to Be Angels: The Class System among the Cherokees at the Female Seminary," *American Indian Culture and Research Journal* 15 (1991), 29–52; L. DeAne Langerquist, *In America the Men Milk the Cows: Factors of Gender, Ethnicity, and Religion in the Americanization of Norwegian-American Women* (Brooklyn, 1992); and Susan Lee Johnson, "'A Memory Sweet to Soldiers': The Significance of Gender in the History of the 'American West,'" *Western Historical Quarterly* 24.4 (November 1993), 495–517. For further discussion of differentiations, see Cynthia Fuchs Epstein, *Deceptive Distinctions: Sex, Gender, and the Social Order* (New Haven, 1988); and Sandra Lipsitz Bem, *The Lenses of Gender: Transforming the Debate on Sexual Inequality* (New Haven, 1993).

41. In discussions of race and feminist theory, the term *race* usually denotes only African-Americans. See, for example, Carrie Jane Singleton, "Race and Gender in Feminist Theory," *Sage* 6 (Summer 1989), 12–17; and Nancie E. Caraway, "The Challenge and Theory of Feminist Identity Politics: Working on Racism," *Frontiers* 12 (Spring 1991), 109–29, and *Segregated Sisterhood: Racism and the Politics of American Feminism* (Knoxville, 1991). For a review of developments in black, non-western women's history. see Cheryl Townsend Gilkes, "Dual Heroisms and Double Burdens: Interpreting Afro-American Women's Experience and History," *Feminist Studies* 15 (Fall 1989), 573–90.

42. Anne M. Butler, "Still in Chains: Black Women in Western Prisons, 1865–1910," *Western Historical Quarterly* 20 (February 1989), 14–36; and Glenda Riley, "American Daughters: Black Women in the West," *Montana, The Magazine of Western History* 38 (Spring 1988), 14–27.

43. Lynn M. Hudson, "A New Look, or 'I'm Not Mammy to Everybody in California': Mary Ellen Pleasant, a Black Entrepreneur," *Journal of the West* 32 (July 1993), 35–40; and Paul R. Spickard, "Work and Hope: African American Women in Southern California during World War II," *Journal of the West* 33 (July 1993), 70–

79. In the more popular realm, Loren Katz, author of *The Black West*, 3d ed. (Seattle, 1987), is working on a pictorial history of black women in the West, which may in turn encourage further scholarly work.

44. See David Beesley, "From Chinese to Chinese American: Chinese Women and Families in a Sierra Nevada Town," *California History* 67 (September 1988), 168–79; Wesley S. Woo, "Presbyterian Mission: Christianizing and Civilizing the Chinese in Nineteenth Century California," *American Presbyterians* 68 (Fall 1990), 167–78; Sucheng Chan, *Entry Denied: Exclusion and the Chinese Community in America, 1882–1943* (Philadelphia, 1991); Gail M. Nomura, "Significant Lives: Asians and Asian Americans in the History of the U.S. West," *Western Historical Quarterly* 25 (Spring 1994), 69–88.

45. Eleanor C. Nordyke and Richard K. C. Lee, "The Chinese in Hawai'i: A Historical and Demographic Perspective," *Hawaiian Journal of History* 23 (1989), 196–216; and Teresa K. Williams, "Marriage between Japanese Women and U.S. Servicemen since World War II," *Amerasia Journal* 17 (1991), 135–54.

46. See Richard White, *"It's Your Misfortune and None of My Own": A New History of the American West* (Norman, 1990). For a fuller discussion of the "new" western history, see Patricia Nelson Limerick, Clyde A. Milner II, and Charles E. Rankin, eds., *Trails: Toward a New Western History* (Lawrence, 1991).

47. Kathleen Underwood, "The Pace of Their Own Lives: Teacher Training and the Life Course of Western Women," *Pacific Historical Review* 55 (November 1986), 513–30; and Dorothy Schwieder, "Education and Change in the Lives of Iowa Farm Women, 1900–1940," *Agricultural History* 60 (Spring 1986), 200–215.

48. Susan L. Allen, "Progressive Spirit: The Oklahoma and Indian Territory Federation of Women's Clubs," *Chronicles of Oklahoma* 66 (Spring 1988), 4–21; Glenda Riley, "Women's Responses to the Challenges of Plains Living," *Great Plains Quarterly* 9 (Summer 1989), 174–84; Mary Lou Locke, "Out of the Shadows and into the Western Sun: Working Women of the Late Nineteenth-Century Urban Far West," *Journal of Urban History* 16 (February 1990), 175–204; Sherilyn Cox Bennion, *Equal to the Occasion: Women Editors of the Nineteenth-Century West* (Reno, 1990); Barbara J. Burt-Way, "Gender and Sustaining Political Ambition: A Study of Arizona Elected Officials," *Western Political Quarterly* 45 (March 1992), 11–25; and Sandra Schackel, *Social Housekeepers: Women Shaping Public Policy in New Mexico, 1920–1940* (Albuquerque, 1992).

49. Another example is, Joanne E. Passet, *Cultural Crusaders: Women Librarians in the American West, 1900-1917* (Albuquerque, 1994).

50. Nancy Shoemaker, "The Rise or Fall of Iroquois Women," *Journal of Women's History* 2 (Winter 1991), 39–57; and Devon A. Mihesuah, *Cultivating the Rosebuds: The Education of Women at the Cherokee Female Seminary, 1851–1909* (Urbana, 1993).

51. Janet D. Spector, *What This Awl Means: Feminist Archaeology at a Wahpeton Dakota Village* (St. Paul, 1993). A similar trend in Latina history is seen in Ruiz, *Cannery Women, Cannery Lives*; Patricia Zavella, "The Impact of 'Sun-Belt' Industrialization on Chicanas," Working Paper Series No. 7, Stanford University Center for Chicano Research (September 1984), 1–25; and Irene Ledesma, *Unlikely Strikers: Mexican-American Women in Strike Activity in Texas, 1919–1974* (Ph.D. diss., Ohio State University, 1992).

52. Carol Devens, *Countering Colonization: Native American Women and Great Lakes Missions, 1630–1900* (Berkeley, 1992). For similar trends among western women of color, see Vicki L. Ruiz, "Dead Ends or Gold Mines?" in Vicki L. Ruiz and Susan Tiano, eds., *Women on the U.S.–Mexico Border: Responses to Change* (Boulder, 1991); and Peggy Pascoe, "Gender Systems in Conflict: The Marriages of Mission-Educated Chinese American Women, 1874–1939," *Journal of Social History* 22 (Fall/Summer 1988–1989), 631–52.

53. Leela Gulati, "Understanding Social Forces through Individual Lives: Case Study as a Research Method," *Manushi* 65 (January/February 1991), 14–17. See also David Morgan, "Masculinity, Autobiography and History," *Gender and History* 2 (Spring 1990), 34–39; and Gloria Steinem, "Seeking Out the Invisible Woman," *New York Times* (March 13, 1992), c1, c16.

54. See John S. Gray, "The Story of Mrs. Picotte-Galpin, A Sioux Heroine," *Montana, The Magazine of Western History* 36 (Summer 1986), 2–21; Kathryn Anderson, "Anne Martin and the Dream of Political Equality for Women," *Journal of the West* 27 (April 1988), 28–34; Beverly Beeton, "'I Am an American Woman': Charlotte Ives Cobb Godbe Kirby," *Journal of the West* 27 (April 1988), 13–19; Joan Mark, *A Stranger in Her Native Land: Alice Fletcher and the American Indians* (Lincoln, 1988); and Sally M. Miller, *From Prairie to Prison: The Life of Social Activist Kate Richards O'Hare* (Columbia, Mo., 1993).

55. Ruth Barnes Moynihan, *Rebel for Rights: Abigail Scott Duniway* (New Haven, 1985); Anderson, "Anne Martin and the Dream," *Journal of the West* 27 (April 1988), 28–34; Norton B. Stern, "Harriet Ashim Choynski, An 1850 Western Arrival," *Western States Jewish History* 24 (April 1991), 214–20; Michael Allen, "The Rise and Decline of the Rodeo Cowgirl: The Career of Mabel Strickland, 1916–1941," *Pacific Northwest Quarterly* 83 (October 1993), 122–27; Shirl Kasper, *Annie Oakley* (Norman, 1992).

56. For discussions of women's biography, see Jean Baker, "Writing Female Lives: The Case of Mary Todd Lincoln," *The Psychohistory Review* 17 (Fall 1988), 34–48; Personal Narratives Group, ed., *Interpreting Women's Lives: Feminist Theory and Personal Narratives* (Bloomington, 1989); Louise A. Tilly, "Gender, Women's History, and Social History," *Social Science History* 13 (Winter 1989), 439–80; Peter Stansky, "The Crumbling Frontier of History and Biography: Some Personal Remarks," *Pacific Historical Review* 61 (February 1990), 1–14; Kathleen Barry, "The New Historical Syntheses: Women's Biography," *Journal of Women's History* 1 (Winter 1990), 77–105; Liz Stanley, "Moments of Writing: Is There a Feminist Auto/biography?" *Gender and History* 2 (Spring 1990), 58–67; Sara Alpern, Joyce Antler, Elisabeth Israels Perry, and Ingrid Winther Scobie, eds., *The Challenge of Feminist Biography: Writing the Lives of Modern American Women* (Urbana, 1992); and Carolyn G. Heilbrun, "Is Biography Fiction?" *Soundings* 76 (Summer/Fall 1993), 293–304.

57. See, for example, Glenda Riley, *The Life and Legacy of Annie Oakley* (Norman, 1994).

58. Valerie Sherer Mathes, *Helen Hunt Jackson and Her Indian Reform Legacy* (Austin, 1990), xiii–xiv, and "The California Mission Indian Commission of 1891: The Legacy of Helen Hunt Jackson," *California History* (Winter 1993–94), 338–59;

Julie Roy Jeffrey, *Converting the West: A Biography of Narcissa Whitman* (Norman, 1991); and Shirley A. Leckie, *Elizabeth Bacon Custer and the Making of a Myth* (Norman, 1993), xix–xxi.

59. Peggy Pascoe, *Relations of Rescue: The Search for Female Moral Authority in the American West, 1874–1939* (New York, 1990). See also Cornelia Butler Flora and Jan L. Flora, "Structure of Agriculture and Women's Culture in the Great Plains," *Great Plains Quarterly* 8 (Fall 1988), 195–205; and Peggy Pascoe, "Western Women at the Cultural Crossroads," in Limerick, Milner, and Rankin, *Trails*, 40–58.

60. See Betty García-Bahne, "La Chicana and the Chicano Family," in Sánchez and Cruz, *Essays on La Mujer*, 30–47; Ann Schofield, "The Women's March: Miners, Family, and Community in Pittsburg, Kansas, 1921–1922," *Kansas History* 7 (Summer 1984), 159–68; Harris, "Sex Roles and Work Patterns"; and Pascoe, "Gender Systems in Conflict.

61. Virginia Scharff, "Gender and Western History: Is Anybody Home on the Range?" *Montana, The Magazine of Western History* 41 (Spring 1991), 62–65.

62. Peggy Pascoe, "Race, Gender, and Intercultural Relations: The Case of Interracial Marriage," *Frontiers* (Winter 1991), 5–18; and Sally M. Miller, "California Immigrants: Case Studies in Continuity and Change in Societal and Familial Roles," *Journal of the West* 33 (July 1993), 25–34.

63. Paula Petrik, "If She Be Content: The Development of Montana Divorce Law, 1865–1907," *Western Historical Quarterly* 18 (July 1987), 261–92; Glenda Riley, "Torn Asunder: Divorce in Early Oklahoma Territory," *Chronicles of Oklahoma* 777 (Winter 1989–90), 61–71, and "Sara Bard Field, Charles Erskine Wood and the Phenomenon of Migratory Divorce," *California History* 69 (Fall 1990), 250–59; Susan Gonda, "Not a Matter of Choice: San Diego Women and Divorce, 1850–1880," *Journal of San Diego History* 37 (Summer 1991), 194–213.

64. Two recent studies of western children are Elliott West, *Growing Up with the Country: Childhood on the Far Western Frontier* (Albuquerque, 1989); and Elizabeth Hampsten, *Settlers' Children: Growing Up on the Great Plains* (Norman, 1991). Other examples are George N. Otey, "New Deal for Oklahoma's Children: Federal Day Care Centers, 1933–1946," *Chronicles of Oklahoma* 62 (Fall 1984), 296–311; Gilbert G. González, "Segregation of Mexican Children in a Southern California City: The Legacy of Expansionism and the American Southwest," *Western Historical Quarterly* 16 (January 1985), 55–76; Sara A. Brown and Robie O. Sargent, "Children in the Sugar Beet Fields of the North Platte Valley of Nebraska, 1923," *Nebraska History* 67 (Fall 1986), 256–303; and James H. Conrad, "Aid to Families with Dependent Children in Texas, 1941–1981," in Frank Annunziata et al., eds., *For the General Welfare: Essays in Honor of Robert H. Bremner* (New York, 1989), 337–60.

65. Charles R. King, "The Woman's Experience of Childbirth on the Western Frontier," *Journal of the West* 29 (January 1990), 76–84; Mary Melcher, "Women's Matters: Birth Control, Prenatal Care, and Childbirth in Rural Montana, 1910–1940," *Montana, The Magazine of Western History* 41 (Spring 1991), 47–56; and Deborah Fink and Alicia Carriquiry, "Having Babies or Not: Household Composition and Fertility in Rural Iowa and Nebraska, 1900–1910," *Great Plains Quarterly* (Summer 1992), 157–68.

66. Glenda Riley, *Building and Breaking Families in the American West* (Albuquerque, 1996).

67. Paula A. Treckel, "An Historiographical Essay: Women on the American Frontier," *Old Northwest* 1 (December 1975), 391–403; Jensen and Miller, "Gentle Tamers Revisited," 173–214; Sandra L. Myres, "Women in the West," in Michael P. Malone, ed., *Historians and the American West* (Lincoln, 1983), 369–86; and Glenda Riley, "Women on the Great Plains: Recent Developments in Research," *Great Plains Quarterly* 5 (Spring 1985), 81–92.

68. For historiography, see Lillian S. Robinson, "Sometimes, Always, Never: Their Women's History and Ours," *New Literary History* 2 (Winter 1990), 377–93. For the gender-history issue, see, for example, Gisela Bock, "Women's History and Gender History: Aspects of an International Debate," *Gender and History* 1 (Spring 1989), 7–30; Jane Sherron De Hart, "Women's History, Gender History, and Political History," *The Public Historian* 15 (Fall 1993), 77–88; Kathleen M. Brown, "Brave New Worlds: Women's and Gender History," *William and Mary Quarterly* 50 (April 1993), 311–28. For deconstruction, see Linda K. Kerber, "Separate Spheres, Female Worlds, Woman's Place: The Rhetoric of Women's History," *Journal of American History* 75 (June/September 1988), 9–39; and Louise M. Newman, "Critical Theory and the History of Women: What's at Stake in Deconstructing Women's History," *Journal of Women's History* 2 (Winter 1991), 58–108. For socialism, see Elizabeth Fox-Genovese, "Socialist-Feminist American Women's History," *Journal of Women's History* 1 (Winter 1990), 181–210. For women's "everyday life," see Julia Swindells, "Hanging Up on Mum or Questions of Everyday Life in the Writing of History," *Gender and History* 2 (Spring 1990), 68–78; and Elaine J. Lawless, "Women's Life Stories and Reciprocal Ethnography as Feminist and Emergent," *Journal of Folklore Research* 28 (January/April 1991), 35–60. For interdisciplinary approaches, see Ruth-Ellen Boetcher Joeres and Barbara Laslett, "Looking Backward, Looking Forward," *Signs* 16 (Spring 1991), 433–40. For multiculturalism, see Elsa Barkley Brown, "Mothers of Mind," *Sage* 6 (Summer 1989), 4–11; and Christine Di Stefanco, "Who the Heck Are We? Theoretical Turns against Gender," *Frontiers* 12 (Spring 1990), 86–108. For the future of women's history, see Gerda Lerner, "Priorities and Challenges in Women's History Research," *Perspectives* 26 (April 1988), 17–20.

69. See Susan Armitage, "Common Ground: Introduction to 'American Women's Narratives,'" *Women's Studies* 14 (1987), 1–4; Gayle R. Davis, "Women's Frontier Diaries: Writing for Good Reason," *Women's Studies* 14 (1987), 5–14; and Judy Nolte Lensink, "Expanding the Boundaries of Criticism: The Diary as Female Autobiography," *Women's Studies* 14 (1987), 39–45. For more general discussions, see Suzanne L. Bunkers, "Diaries: Public and Private Records of Women's Lives," *Legacy* 7 (Fall 1990), 17–26; and Andrew P. Norman, "Telling It Like It Was: Historical Narratives on Their Own Terms," *History and Theory* 30 (Spring 1991), 119–35.

70. John Mack Faragher, "Twenty Years of Western Women's History," *Montana, The Magazine of Western History* 41 (Spring 1991), 71–73; and Glenda Riley, "Continuity and Change: Interpreting Women in Western History," *Journal of the West* 32 (July 1993), 7–11.

71. George A. Peffer, "From under the Sojourner's Shadow: A Historiographical

Study of Chinese Female Immigration to America, 1852–1882," *Journal of American Ethnic History* 11 (Spring 1992), 41–67.

72. Betty J. Harris, "Ethnicity and Gender in the Global Periphery: A Comparison of Basotho and Navajo Women," *American Indian Culture and Research Journal* 14 (1990), 15–38; Peggy Pascoe, "Introduction: The Challenge of Writing Multicultural Women's History," *Frontiers* 12 (Fall 1991), 1–4; Sarah Deutsch, "Coming Together, Coming Apart—Women's History and the West," *Montana, The Magazine of Western History* 41 (Spring 1991), 58–61; Judy Nolte Lensink, "Beyond the Intellectual Meridian: Transdisciplinary Studies of Women," *Pacific Historical Review* 61 (November 1992), 463–80; Pascoe, "Western Women at the Cultural Crossroads," in Limerick, Milner, and Rankin, *Trails*, 44–58.

73. Virginia Scharff, "Else Surely We Shall All Hang Separately: The Politics of Western Women's History," *Pacific Historical Review* 61 (November 1992), 535–56; Glenda Riley, "Western Women's History: A Look at Some of the Issues," *Montana, The Magazine of Western History* 41 (Spring 1991), 66–70; and Susan H. Armitage, "Revisiting 'The Gentle Tamers Revisited': The Problems and Possibilities of Western Women's History," *Pacific Historical Review* 61 (November 1992), 459–62.

74. Susan H. Koester, "'By the Words of Thy Mouth Let Thee Be Judged': The Alaska Native Sisterhood Speaks," *Journal of the West* 27 (April 1988), 35–44; and John S. Whitehead, "The Anti-Statehood Movement of the Legacy of Alice Kamokila Campbell," *Hawaiian Journal of History* 27 (1993), 43–63.

75. Devens, *Countering Civilization*, 24.

76. Jan C. Dawson, "Sacagawea: Pilot or Pioneer Mother?" *Pacific Northwest Quarterly* 83 (January 1992), 22–28.

77. Richard White, "Race Relations in the American West," *American Quarterly* 38 (1986), 406.

Part 2
Analysis
and Methodology

4
Writing the Ethnohistory of Native Women

Theda Perdue

In 1757 Attakullakulla, a distinguished Cherokee headman, appeared before the South Carolina governor's council. Gazing around the room, he appeared startled, and he asked the governor why there were no women in attendance. After all, he pointed out to the governor, "White Men as well as the Red were born of Women."[1] Attakullakulla was accustomed to seeing women in council meetings and hearing their views. Although political inclusiveness like that practiced by the Cherokees was far from universal in native North America, women did have central roles in native societies. Uncovering those roles and the ways in which they have changed over time poses a major challenge to ethnohistorians. Equally daunting is the task of determining what sort of impact gender and perceptions of gender may have had on shaping native societies and interaction between natives and non-natives. Since policies, both native and colonial, rested on assumptions about the people toward whom they were directed, gender must have figured into the equation. The absence of women in the South Carolina council, after all, helped shape Attakullakulla's view of the British; his expectations shaped British views of Cherokees.[2]

As ethnohistorians, we rely largely on written records. Until the nineteenth century, Europeans generated most written records relating to native peoples. For this reason, ethnohistorians constantly confront the problem of how to write a people's cultural history when outsiders, and often hostile outsiders, wrote the documents on which we must rely. We try to solve the problem by using theoretical models from anthropology and other social sciences, archaeological evidence, linguistics, and oral traditions. The documents, however, still remain at the core of what we do. The complicating factor in writing the ethnohistory of native women is that European men, not women, wrote the vast majority of documents. Many of the encounters that produced documents, in particular trade relations and military alliances, involved native men far more than women.[3] Circumstances surrounding two other major bodies of evidence—mission records and travel accounts— also limit their usefulness. As purposeful bearers of European culture, missionaries were particularly culture-bound, and travelers often did not linger long enough with any group of people to penetrate the formal, public side of culture.

There are some notable exceptions to male authorship—captivity narratives; reports of missionaries, teachers, and reservation matrons; and letters and journals of pioneer women.[4] Most of these women, however, stood apart from native societies.[5] Accepting previously formulated views of native women that linked "savagery" with heightened sexuality, they were terrified that they might become tainted by too close association. Men, on the other hand, were more likely to become enmeshed in native society: natural historians and other supposedly objective observers pried into a variety of practices, traders married native women and raised families, and government officials became involved in political life. But these men generally had little interest in native women beyond the food they produced or the sex they provided, and consequently they left few references to women or women's lives. They considered women to be less important than men, and in any event, the concerns of women were not concerns of theirs.

Even if male European observers had been interested in the economic, social, political, and ritual lives of women, they would have encountered considerable difficulty in gaining access. Native men and women lived remarkably separate lives. A sexual division of labor underlay much of this separation. Men and women performed different tasks: in most of North America, men hunted while women farmed and/or gathered. Even the most notable exception, agricultural peoples in the Southwest, fits the pattern in some ways. While men cultivated the corn among the Hopi and Zuni, for example, women had the laborious task of preparing it for consumption, and the production of corn as well as humans was understood to rest with women.[6] Task defined gender among native people, and a woman could not fill the role of a man and remain an ordinary woman. Similarly, a man who worked alongside women in the fields crossed genders and became something other than a man.[7] Consequently, few men—native or non-native—learned techniques for making corn grow; they did not know the rituals or the corn songs that belonged to women. Task differentiation often extended to spatial separation, that is, men and women did not work in the same places. In *What This Awl Means: Feminist Archaeology at a Wahpeton Dakota Village*, Janet Spector suggests that for three months (March through May), men and women even lived in separate camps as men hunted muskrats and women made sugar.[8] Furthermore, tools seem to have been task and, therefore, gender specific, a distinction that increased the distance between men and women.

Social divisions also existed. In her ethnographic novel, *Waterlily*, Ella Cara Deloria described conversation and seating arrangements in a Dakota tipi. Waterlily and her husband, Sacred Horse, had called on the parents of Red Leaf, who had become fictive kin to Waterlily in her husband's camp.

> The dog barked a warning and a man outside called, "Do you sit there?" "Yes, come in," said Red Leaf's father. (Men replied to men, women to women.) The woman of the tipi was saying, "Let me see . . . oh yes, there is plenty of stew left. (Tilting her kettle to look) He never wants much, late at night—just a snack . . ." while the husband was saying, "That's Yankton, the camp circle crier, you know. He is our friend. He always drops in to see us at this time." Husband and wife spoke simultaneously. Waterlily caught both remarks.
>
> She and Sacred Horse had been sitting side by side in the honor-place. But now the men and women formed two distinct groups, according to sex. People always tended to do this unconsciously. Waterlily eased over toward the mother and Sacred Horse toward the father. Yankton joined the men on the left side of the tipi.[9]

Even when men and women did not speak at the same time to their respective genders or sit on opposite sides, important distinctions remained.

Men had an even more difficult time in gaining access to women's ceremonies than to their economic or social life. Women's ritual life focused on reproduction. While some cultures, particular the Athapascan-speaking peoples (Apaches and Navajos) of the Southwest, publicly celebrated a girl's first menstruation, many native peoples regarded menstruating women as powerful and dangerous. Consequently, native women usually sequestered themselves during their menses, bathed ritually, meditated, fasted, and performed other rituals to heighten spirituality. Unlike Speaker of the House Newt Gingrich, who explained his opposition to women in the military in terms of the "infections" women suffer every thirty days, native people did not regard menstruation as a malady. Instead, practices regarding menstruation stemmed from respect and even fear. As Thomas Buckley pointed out in an article on the Yurok of northern California, men performed similar rites when seeking visions or spiritual purity.[10] Men closed their rituals to women; by the same token, women excluded men. Consequently, male European observers never had access to most female ceremonialism, particularly that relating to menstruation. Furthermore, European cultural views of menstruation as shameful made it unlikely that European women, had they had the opportunity to participate, would have availed themselves of it.

The documents on which historians rely, therefore, are often silent on women; women are nearly as absent from historical records as colonial women were from the South Carolina council. Consequently, historical writing often marginalizes women. One can gauge the peripheralization of women through the indexes of works in Native American history, even fairly enlightened ones.[11] One of the topics typically indexed is "women," a subject covered sufficiently to merit an entry. "Men," on the other hand, have no such entry because the story that is being told is the story of men.

Anthropologists are less wedded to written documents than historians and rely more heavily on observation, even though they may be primarily interested in the ancestors of the modern people whom they observe.[12] Ethnohistorians look to anthropologists, in particular, to alert them to the culturally significant information that their documentary sources may contain. This reliance is not without its own set of problems. Most of the ethnographic data about native peoples used by ethnohistorians was collected in the late nineteenth and early twentieth centuries. During this period, Indians seemed to be vanishing. Confined to reservations or allotted individual homesteads, Native Americans, many people believed, would either die out physically or be assimilated by the dominant culture. The "disappearance" of Indians coincided with the emergence of anthropology as an academic discipline, and anthropologists rushed to record what was left of the cultural traditions of native peoples before they faded from view. Early anthropologists compared "primitive" customs, that is, native behavior, to "civilized" practices, that is, their own. Furthermore, they equated Indians to the impoverished people in their own societies. Alice Kehoe has described the consequences of this approach for native women: "The traditional picture of the Plains Indian woman is really that of an Irish housemaid of the late Victorian era clothed in a buckskin dress."[13] The apparent discrepancy between the amount of work women did and that performed by men led to the belief that native women were oppressed and degraded, the virtual slaves of men. For the ethnohistorian, the result is valuable observations flawed by incredibly ethnocentric interpretations.

The "primitive"/"civilized" dichotomy gave way to other paradigms that focused on the internal structures of native societies, but comparisons remained intrinsic to the discipline: that is, anthropologists continued to explain other cultures in order to make them intelligible to their own. By focusing on the differences between cultures, anthropologists often missed or gave too little weight to differences among the people within the cultures they were studying.[14] Frequently, anthropologists simply overlooked gender in general and women in particular. Claude Lévi-Strauss has become infamous, for example, for his observation: "The entire village left the next day in about 30 canoes, leaving us alone with the women and children in the abandoned houses."[15]

Archaeologists have ignored women in similar ways. In the late nineteenth and early twentieth centuries, amateurs obsessed with collecting dominated the excavation of most North American sites. Organized into gentlemen's clubs, these collectors focused their attention on the recovery of artifacts rather than the reconstruction of societies, and some even moved beyond amateurism and became artifactual entrepreneurs.[16] The Choctaw Mining Company, for example, brought in heavy equipment and hired crews to unearth the treasures of the Spiro mound site in eastern Oklahoma. These collectors sought stone and shell artifacts, in particular, and ceramics secondarily, and they largely ignored other types of artifactual evidence. Even if they had been so inclined, few ways to identify and analyze plant remains existed. They associated virtually all the artifacts they recovered with men and male activities and, therefore, men emerged as the dominant and most productive members of the community.[17] Archaeology seemed to corroborate an anthropological view of men as active and women as passive, a dichotomy presented in anthropology textbooks well into the 1960s.[18] As late as 1986, with much theory and little evidence, archaeologist Guy Prentice attributed the initial cultivation and domestication of plants to men because they controlled commerce and ceremony and, implicitly, innovation.[19]

Although anthropology and archaeology historically have only reinforced the notion of male dominance, over the last twenty years anthropology, in particular, has provided us with a way out of the androcentric, or male-centered, morass in which academic disciplines have been trapped. Feminist anthropologists began to assert that gender itself is a cultural construction.[20] Culture rather than strictly biology defines what it means to be a "woman" or a "man." Because cultures vary enormously, the cultural definitions and expectations of men and women also vary. In *Feminism and Anthropology*, Henrietta Moore argued that "an understanding of gender relations must remain central to the analysis of key questions in anthropology and in the social sciences as a whole."[21] Janet Spector suggested that archaeologists might gender their analysis of artifacts through task differentiation, that is, through determining which tasks women performed, which tasks men performed, and which artifacts related to the tasks of each. In order to do so, archaeologists must rely on the ethnographic literature describing division of labor in historic native societies. Her own analysis of ethnographic data on the Hidatsa, like her later research on the Wahpeton, revealed that men and women led very separate lives. Recognition of that separation and its reflection in the artifacts, she argued, not only humanizes archaeology but also makes it less androcentric.[22] In his excavation of Tukabatchee, a historic Creek town with deep Mississippian roots, Vernon James Knight discovered that household arrangement seemed to conform to the pattern described by the eighteenth-century natural historian William Bartram, in which structures surrounded a central courtyard. The artifacts he found, however, were not distributed equally among the structures. By analyzing artifacts with reference to what we know about Creek division of labor, he was able to identify certain sections of a household as women's areas and others as men's.[23] According to Spector, such spatial, task, and tool differentiation implies that men and women knew little about each other's work and, consequently, exercised little control over it. The result is considerable gender autonomy, and the implication is a worldview in which men balance women rather than the European conception of a hierarchical universe in which men rank above women.

Anthropologists and archaeologists, like historians, must overcome not only the legacy of their disciplines, but also their own ethnocentrism. In a paper delivered to the Southeastern Archaeological Conference, Patricia Galloway urged her colleagues to suppress their ethnocentric squeamishness about menstruation and look for menstrual huts and for ceremonial objects associated with women. Such data not only promises insight into the lives of women, but this kind of material evidence can provide clues to the social and political structure of Mississippian chiefdoms.[24] The study of women and of gender, therefore, can lead us to revise our views of broader scholarly issues.

In order to combat ethnocentrism in our own work, we can take a new look at old materials and ferret out what is useful in them. When Lt. Henry Timberlake, one of the British soldiers stationed at Fort Loudoun in east Tennessee in the 1750s, hired a woman as his agent for purchasing corn for the garrison, he revealed not only the importance of corn to the Cherokee economy and the fort, but indicated who controlled corn. In 1802, however, a party surveying the boundary between North Carolina and the Cherokee Nation procured virtually all its food, including corn and bread, from men rather than women.[25] A profound cultural change, with particular reference to women, had taken place.

The traditional social separation of men and women and the ways in which cultural norms shaped change are detectable in other ways. In Muskogean as well as other languages, for example, men and women did not use the same words for some things.[26] When the Spanish introduced cattle to the Choctaws in the eighteenth century, for example, men incorporated the Spanish word *vaca* into their vocabulary. Women, however, applied the same Choctaw word that they used for fruit trees. Changes in the Choctaw language reflect broader historical change: cattle gradually replaced deerskins as an item men traded to outsiders, while women prized the milk, butter, and cheese that cows produced, much in the same way that trees bear fruit.[27]

The ritual life of women, while even more obscure in historical sources, can nevertheless be inferred. Travelers, in particular, frequently noted the presence of "menstrual huts," or women's houses, where these rituals took place.[28] Europeans usually interpreted seclusion and avoidance as stemming from a native belief that menstruating women were "unclean." If they had paid attention to native mythology, however, they would have discovered the spiritual significance of menstruation and the great power with which it imbued women. Among people as diverse as the Illinois of the Midwest and the Yurok of California, women sought visions during their seclusion.[29] This experience did not differ dramatically from the vision quests of men in many native cultures, nor does the isolation itself seem radically different from the seclusion sought by men before and after engaging in warfare. For women as well as men, the purpose was spiritual, not hygienic. A Cherokee myth reveals the power of menstruating women. Stone Man was a spiritual being who preyed on lone hunters until the Cherokees managed to destroy him by stationing seven menstruating women in his path.[30]

The Cherokees associated blood with creation and reproduction. In their mythology corn sprang from the blood of Selu, the first woman.[31] Most native people mythically linked the earth's origin, its peopling, and their sustenance to a woman. Iroquois accounts of the creation usually contain a woman who fell from the sky, landed on the back of a turtle, created the earth, planted crops, and gave birth to a daughter whose own children become the creators of man.[32] Seclusion, fasting, meditating, and ritual bathing during menstruation connected women to their mythic past and their spiritual powers. It is possible, therefore, to overcome some of the gender bias in historical documents.

Much of our information about traditional beliefs comes from early ethnographers whose work, as we already have seen, reflected profound ethnocentrism. Some of these ethnographers took particular interest in women, and while their interpretations may be seriously flawed, the information they provided is invaluable. Documenting relatively ordinary women with a focus on the tasks they performed and the personal events—menarche, marriage, and childbirth—that shaped their lives, such works can contribute to a more inclusive Native American history. *Waheenee: An Indian Girl's Story*, told by herself to Gilbert L. Wilson, is one example.[33] Waheenee, or Buffalo-Bird Woman, was a Hidatsa woman born about 1839 in a village near where the Knife River enters the Missouri, in what is today North Dakota. When she was six years old, her people relocated up the Missouri River valley to land that is now part of the Fort Berthold Reservation. For ten years, beginning in 1908, Waheenee acted as one of the chief informants for Wilson, an anthropologist from the American Museum of Natural History. She told Wilson about her childhood, the stories she heard and the games she played, her relatives, the earth lodges in which her people lived, training dogs, accompanying buffalo-hunting parties, planting and harvesting corn, picking berries, getting married, becoming a widow, remarrying, having a child, and growing old. Her life was hard in many ways, but it was also rewarding. "We cared for our corn in those days, as we would care for a child," Waheenee recalled, "for we Indian people loved our fields as mothers love their children. We thought that the corn plants had souls, as children have souls, and that the growing corn liked to hear us sing, as children like to hear their mothers sing to them."[34]

Waheenee's recollections suggest a very different native woman than the drudge that travelers and even some of Wilson's colleagues described. Proud of what she did, Waheenee was self-confident and unapologetic about her life as a Hidatsa woman. In addition to broadening our understanding of native societies, the inclusion of women like Waheenee in our histories can act as a corrective to stereotypes of native people. The Indian hunter and warrior—the man—projects an image of native people as unsettled and threatening. Women planting crops, singing their corn songs, cleaning skins, and looking after children present a contradictory image of Indians as stable, hardworking, joyful, and caring.

The lives of extraordinary women, who succeeded in areas normally associated with men, can also be instructive. Some of these women crossed gender lines completely and permanently, while others merely assumed unusual roles.[35] In "Cockacoeske, Queen of Pamunkey: Diplomat and Suzeraine,"[36] Martha W. McCartney documented the achievements of a woman with considerable political authority. In my own essay on the Cherokee War Woman, Nancy Ward,[37] I explored the structures within a culture that permitted some women to participate in pursuits normally reserved to men and concluded that the Cherokees simply created a new category, War Woman, for women who distinguished themselves in war in order to preserve normal gender conventions. Other scholars, including Evelyn Blackwood, Paula Gunn Allen,[38] and Beatrice Medicine,[39] have looked at women who permanently crossed genders and became men, sexually as well as in all other ways. Medicine related a trader's account of a Gros Ventre woman, who had been adopted by the Crows and trained in male skills. She dressed like a woman, but she was a "proficient hunter" and a "skilled warrior." She sat with the men in council, ranked as the third leading warrior, and acquired four wives. Medicine observed, "Although this woman's manly-oriented life may have been exceptional, it was socially recognized and esteemed among the people with whom she lived." The study of such women supports the contention that gender is culturally constructed, and by using circumstances where contradictions arise (women succeed at things that only men are supposed to do, or culturally defined men menstruate), this research moves us closer to identifying gender systems and the role of gender. The ultimate result of this approach may be a new Native American history.

In 1971, Robert F. Berkhofer, Jr., called for a new Indian history written from a Native American perspective.[40] He suggested that one way to develop an Indian-centered history was to examine "the nature of political organization in a so-called tribe and the role it plays in Indian–Indian and Indian–white relations."[41] The way Berkhofer proposed to go about this was through an examination of factionalism, which, he maintained, "figures so prominently in past and present Indian life that the historian, regardless of ignorance, must reckon with its effects for both the interpretation and evaluation of sources."[42] Nevertheless, Berkhofer acknowledged that "the political view of Indian history, while crucial to its interpretation, is only one way of looking at persistence and change in the story of American Indians."[43] I suggest that another way is gender, a cultural construct that is at least as intrinsic as politics and perhaps even subsumes it. But how do we go about studying gender? What expression of gender, like factionalism in politics, can we use to focus our historical analysis?

One possibility is kinship. An analysis of how kinship changes and the relationship of those changes to historical events can reorient our thinking about the past. Anthropologist John H. Moore, in "Dialectics of Cheyenne Kinship: Variability and Change,"[44] traced the shift of the southern Cheyenne from matrilocal buffalo hunters to patrilocal raiders, to ambilocal reservation dwellers. Moore tied major events in Indian–white relations to significant adaptive changes within Cheyenne society. In "War and Culture: The Iroquois Experience," Daniel Richter enhanced our understanding of Iroquois warfare, a political act, by placing it in the context of the kinship system: rather than imperial wars, the Iroquois fought "mourning wars" to avenge the deaths of their relatives.[45]

Another possibility for gendering the past is economic history. By examining the division of labor in native societies and the impact of historical processes and events on the tasks of men and women, we may be able to arrive at a clearer understanding about what change meant to *all* native people.

In "The Political Economy of Gender: A Nineteenth Century Plains Indian Case Study," Alan Klein charted the impact of commercial buffalo hunting on the societies of northern Plains people (Teton Lakota, Assiniboines, Gros Ventre, and Blackfoot) by looking at how increased hunting affected men and women. The workload of women, who processed the skins, increased dramatically while a class system emerged among men. Successful hunters needed more women and so they married more wives, women of their own people or women taken as captives. With more laborers, these men could become even wealthier. This process favored men over women and individuals over the group.

In my own research on Cherokees in the early nineteenth century, I found that paying attention to what men did and what women did revealed a very different view of the whole society than we previously held.[46] The "civilized" Cherokee republic, a creation of men, wrote a constitution, published a newspaper, and impressed citizens of the United States with how different Cherokees were from other Indians. When I began to look at women and the kinds of records women left, however, I discovered a hidden world of Cherokees living in traditional ways and ignoring the pronouncements of missionaries, United States agents, and even their own supposed leaders. I did this by examining men's and women's work, the roles of men and women in the family, and the ways in which nineteenth-century Cherokees gendered politics.[47]

Gender also can reveal a great deal about the interactions of natives and non-natives in North America. Kathleen M. Brown demonstrated in her essay, "The Anglo–Algonquian Frontier," that assumptions about gender shaped relations between the Jamestown colonists and the Powhatans. The Powhatans saw the English as men without women, and so they fed them, slept with them, and made them dependent on the Powhatans. But the English tried to assert masculine authority over the Powhatans according to English perceptions of proper gender relations. The ultimate result, according to Brown, was that "male roles intensified [on both sides] in ways that appear to have reinforced the patriarchial tendencies of each culture."[48] A gendered analysis such as Brown's enhances our understanding not only of men and women, but of the ways in which natives and newcomers viewed each other and responded to actions that seemed culturally unintelligible.

Women's history is, of course, not the same as a gendered analysis of historical events, but women's history can lead us to a gendered analysis. My research on Cherokee women, for example, has made me sensitive to the gendered rhetoric of removal and has prompted me to examine ways in which gendered perceptions contributed to tension and conflict. The rhetoric of

Indian removal is replete with assumptions about men and women. Georgian Wilson Lumpkin railed: "I believe the earth was formed especially for the cultivation of the ground, and none but civilized men will cultivate the earth to any great extent, or advantage. Therefore, I do not believe a savage race of heathens, found in the occupancy of a large and fertile domain of the country, have any exclusive right to the same, from merely having seen it in the chase, or having viewed it from the mountain top."[49] However self-serving, Lumpkin makes clear that he expected men to farm and regarded their failure to do so as evidence of "savagery." Among the Cherokees, widely regarded as the most "civilized" Indian tribe, most men did not farm: the wealthier, more highly acculturated men who sought to emulate whites by having their wives and daughters tend to home and hearth bought African-American slaves or hired sharecroppers; in more traditional Cherokee families, women continued to farm. In pro-removal rhetoric, the failure of men to farm impugned Cherokee "civilization," condemned the Cherokees to impoverishment, and undermined the Cherokee claim to their homeland. Anglo-American views of gender, of men and women, collided with the ways in which Cherokees gendered their society, and the collision destroyed Cherokee credibility in the eyes of many Anglo-Americans, particularly those in power.

Gender is the most basic form of social organization, yet the analysis of women and men in society is in its infancy. Since traditional history was "men's history," any gendered approach to the past had to begin with women's history. We still have much to do in that domain before we can begin to restructure the way we write ethnohistory, but we seem to be moving in that direction. When we are able to answer Attakullakulla's question "Where are the women?" we will be well on our way to reexamining the past as a whole. At that point, women's history or gender studies will no longer be stepchildren of scholarly inquiry, but intrinsic to a more complex analysis of the interaction between men and women. Such scholarship, in turn, can lead to greater understanding of peoples from vastly different cultures, struggling to make sense of encounters with assumptions so fundamental that it takes centuries before anyone realizes how powerful they are.

Notes

1. *South Carolina Journal*, Minutes, 9 Feb. 1757.
2. See Tom Hatley, *The Dividing Paths: Cherokees and South Carolinians through the Era of Revolution* (New York, 1993), 149–54.
3. Although men dominated the pelt and hide trade, there is considerable evi-

dence for women trading other commodities. For example, see Mary C. Wright, "Economic Development and Native American Women in the Early Nineteenth Century," *American Quarterly* 33 (1981), 525–36; Lucy Eldersveld Murphy, "Autonomy and the Economic Roles of Indian Women of Fox-Wisconsin River Region, 1763–1832," in Nancy Shoemaker, ed., *Negotiators of Change: Historical Perspectives on Native American Women* (New York and London, 1995), 72–89.

4. See, for example, June Namias, *White Captives: Gender and Ethnicity on the American Frontier* (Chapel Hill, 1993); Glenda Riley, *Women and Indians on the Frontier, 1825–1915* (Albuquerque, 1984); Theda Perdue, "Southern Indians and the Cult of True Womanhood," in Walter J. Fraser, Jr., R. Frank Saunders, Jr., and Jon L. Wakelyn, eds., *The Web of Southern Social Relations: Women, Family, and Education* (Athens, Ga., 1985); Robert A. Trennert, "Educating Indian Girls at Non-Reservation Boarding Schools, 1878–1920," *Western Historical Quarterly* 13 (1982), 271–90; Lisa E. Emmerich, "'Right in the Midst of My Own People': Native American Women and the Field Matron Program," *American Indian Quarterly* 15 (1991), 201–16.

5. James E. Seaver, *A Narrative of the Life of Mrs. Mary Jemison*, ed. June Namias (Norman, 1992); John Demos, *The Unredeemed Captive: A Family Story from Early America* (New York, 1974).

6. M. Jane Young, "Women, Reproduction, and Religion in Western Puebloan Society," *Journal of American Folklore* 100 (1087), 436–45.

7. The concept of "crossing genders" comes from Evelyn Blackwood, "Sexuality and Gender in Certain Native American Tribes: The Case of Cross-gender Females," *Signs* 10 (1984), 27–42.

8. Janet Spector, *What This Awl Means: Feminist Anthropology at a Wapeton Dakota Village* (St. Paul: Minnesota Historical Society Press, 1993), 73–75.

9. Ella Deloria, *Waterlily* (Lincoln, 1988), 187.

10. Thomas Buckley, "Menstruation and the Power of Yurok Women: Methods in Cultural Reconstruction," *American Ethnologist* 9 (1982), 47–60.

11. For example, see Theda Perdue, *Slavery and the Evolution of Cherokee Society, 1540–1866* (Knoxville, 1979), 207.

12. The best essay on the different approaches of historians and anthropologists remains James Axtell, "Ethnohistory: An Historian's Viewpoint," *Ethnohistory* 26 (1979), 1–13.

13. Alice B. Kehoe, "The Shackles of Tradition," in Patricia Albers and Beatrice Medicine, eds., *The Hidden Half: Studies in Plains Indian Women* (Lanham, Md., 1983), 53–77. She particularly cites Walter McClintock, Alexander Goldenweiser, and Paul Radin.

14. Henrietta L. Moore, *Feminism and Anthropology* (Minneapolis, 1988), 197.

15. Quoted in Alison Wylie, "Gender Theory and the Archaeological Record: Why Is There No Archaeology of Women?" in Joan M. Gero and Margaret W. Conkey, eds., *Engendering Archaeology: Women and Prehistory* (Oxford, 1991), 38.

16. Robert Silverberg, *Mound Builders of Ancient America: The Archaeology of a Myth* (New York, 1968).

17. Joan M. Gero, "Genderlithics: Women's Roles in Stone Tool Production," in Gero and Conkey, *Engendering Archaeology*, 163–93.

18. Patty Jo Watson and Mary C. Kennedy, "The Development of Horticulture in the Eastern Woodlands of North America: Women's Role," in Gero and Conkey, *Engendering Archaeology*, 255–56.

19. Guy Prentice, "Origin of Plant Domestication in the Eastern United States: Promoting the Individual in Archaeological Theory," *Southeastern Archaeology* 5 (1986), 103–9. Watson and Kennedy are reacting to this article in "The Development of Horticulture."

20. Sherry Ortner, "Is Woman to Man as Nature Is to Culture?" in M. Rosaldo and Louise Lamphere, eds., *Woman, Culture, and Society* (Stanford, Calif., 1974), 67–88.

21. Henrietta L. Moore, *Feminism and Anthropology* (Minneapolis: University of Minnesota Press, 1988), 195.

22. "Male/Female Task Differentiation among the Hidatsa: Toward the Development of an Archaeological Approach to the Study of Gender," in Albers and Medicine, *Hidden Half*, 77–100.

23. "Tukabatchee Archaeological Investigations at an Historic Creek Town, Elmore County, Alabama, 1984," Office of Archaeological Research, Alabama State Museum of Natural History, University of Alabama, Report of Investigations 45 (31 July 1985), 116–19.

24. Patricia Galloway, "Where Have All the Menstrual Huts Gone? The Invisibility of Menstrual Seclusion in the Late Prehistoric Southeast," address delivered 1990; revised version presented at the Appalachian State University Conference on Women in Anthropology, 1994.

25. Theda Perdue, "Men, Women and American Indian Policy: The Cherokee Response to 'Civilization,'" in Shoemaker, *Negotiators of Change*, 92, 107.

26. Amelia Rector Bell, "Separate People: Speaking of Creek Men and Women," *American Anthropologist* 92 (1990), 332–45.

27. James T. Carson, "Cattle into Fruit Trees: Gender and Choctaw Incorporation of Livestock," paper presented to the Southern Historical Association, November 1994; forthcoming in *Agricultural History*.

28. For a variety of practices relating to menstruation, see James Axtell, ed., *Indian Peoples of Eastern America: A Documentary History of the Sexes* (New York, 1981), 53–69.

29. Buckley, "Menstruation and the Power of Yurok Women"; from Milo Milton Quaife, ed., *The Western Country in the Seventeenth Century: The Memoirs of Lamothe Cadillac and Pierre Liette* (Chicago, 1947), 132–33; repr. in Axtell, *Indian Peoples of Eastern America*, 57.

30. James Mooney, *Myths of the Cherokees*, 19th Annual Report of the Bureau of American Ethnography (Washington, D.C., 1900), 319–20.

31. Ibid., 244–45.

32. From Hazel W. Hertzberg, *The Great Tree and the Longhouse: The Culture of the Iroquois* (New York, 1966), 12–19; repr. in Axtell, *Indian Peoples of Eastern America*, 173–79.

33. Gilbert L. Wilson, ed., *Waheenee: An Indian Girl's Story* (St. Paul, Minn., 1921; repr. with introduction by Jeffery R. Hanson, Lincoln, 1981).

34. Ibid., 94.

35. The concept of "gender-crossing" is from Evelyn Blackwood, "Sexuality and Gender."

36. In Peter H. Wood, Gregory A. Waselkov, and M. Thomas Hatley, *Powhatan's Mantle: Indians in the Colonial Southeast* (Lincoln, 1989), 173–95.

37. Theda Perdue, "Nancy Ward," in C. J. Barker-Benfield and Catherine Clinton, eds., *Portraits of American Women* (New York, 1991), 83–100.

38. "Lesbians in American Indian Culture," *Conditions* 3 (1981), 67–87.

39. "'Warrior Women—Sex Role Alternatives for Plains Indian Women," in Albers and Medicine, *Hidden Half*, 267–80.

40. "The Political Context of a New Indian History," *Pacific Historical Review* 40 (August 1971), 357–82.

41. Ibid., 368.

42. Ibid., 374.

43. Ibid., 381.

44. John H. Moore, "Dialectics of Cheyenne Kinship: Variability and Change," *Ethnology* 27 (1988), 253–69.

45. Daniel Richter, "War and Culture: The Iroquois Experience," *William and Mary Quarterly* 40 (1983), 528–59.

46. In particular, the one advanced by William G. McLoughlin, *Cherokee Renascence in the New Republic* (Princeton, N.J., 1986).

47. "Women, Men, and American Indian Policy: The Cherokee Response to 'Civilization'" in Shoemaker, *Negotiators of Change*, 90–115; "Women in the Early Cherokee Republic," in Rennard Strickland and Chadwick Smith, eds., *Cherokee History* (forthcoming).

48. In Shoemaker, *Negotiators of Change*, 26–48.

49. *The Removal of the Cherokee Indians from Georgia*, 2 vols. (New York, 1907), 2:150.

5
Indian Peoples
and the Natural World
Asking the Right Questions

Richard White

I

Methodology is at the heart of any historical endeavor because methodology goes directly to the most critical of historical questions: How is that we claim to know about the past? I will make this more specific. Historians concerned with questions of Indians and the environment have made a series of sweeping claims. They have argued that many Indian peoples had, and some still have, quite distinctive ways of understanding and culturally constructing nature and that Indian actions, in fact, shaped much of the North American world that whites regarded as wilderness. How is it that they claim to know this?

In answering this question, we appeal largely to our practice. Academic historians assert knowledge of the past because they agree on a set of methods according to which claims about the past can be evaluated and judged. These methods will ideally yield general, but hardly universal, agreement among practitioners as to whether some claims are more valid or less valid than other claims. Arguably, there may be a consensus on historical methodology in general, but the environmental history of Indian peoples is another, quite separate case. Writing an environmental history of Indian peoples involves a hybrid methodology in which the methods of environmental history meet the methods of Indian history (a.k.a. ethnohistory, a.k.a. anthropological history.) Ethnohistorical methods of cultural reconstruction, scientific methods of landscape reconstruction, and more conventional historical methods all overlap. The result is often dissonance and confusion.

The most basic tasks of any historical method involve asking and answering questions. In any historical methodology, historical methods are intimately related to historical questions. A methodology stipulates not only how to answer questions, but also how to ask them.

Talking about questions in the abstract is confusing, so let me provide as an illustrative text two very broad questions (hereafter Big Question One and Big Question Two) that recur both in the academic and the popular writing about the environment and Indian peoples. They will provide avenues into this methodological issue and prevent the discussion from becoming overly abstract.

First, how do we know what Indians thought in the past about what we now call nature, and what equivalent or related conceptions of the natural world might Indian peoples have had at various times in the past?

Second, How do we know how Indians acted in the past in regard to the natural world, and what were the consequences of their actions?

In answering the first of these questions historians borrow from ethnohistory; in answering the second, they borrow from environmental history and environmental sciences.[1]

How we ask questions is particularly critical in Indian environmental history. It is a field full of pitfalls: hidden assumptions, questions that are really answers in disguise, and loose and unworkable categories. Any methodology that allows us to answer these big questions must stipulate that we ask the questions in a way that makes more than one answer possible. I will call this basic requirement of asking operational questions (that is, questions open to more than one answer) operationality.

To illustrate operationality and the dangers of bad questions, lets go back to Big Question 1.

1. How do we know about what the ancestors of the peoples we now call Indians thought in the past about what we now call nature and what conceptions of the natural world might these ancestors of Indian peoples have had at various times in the past?

This convoluted phrasing might seem to represent an excess of academic caution, the kind of thing that makes it impossible to get a straight answer out of a professor. But the construction is quite purposeful. I want to frame a question that can be answered while at the same time keeping the major concepts the question employs open to interrogation. I am trying *not* to presume too much in the question. I am, in particular, trying not to presume:

First, that there is a universal and transcendent agreement on what "nature" is and that agreement corresponds to our modern concept of nature.

Second, that modern day Indian peoples are identical with or have the same attitudes of their ancestors.

I am also trying to make clear that I *am* acting on a third assumption: that Indians are a people of history and that their beliefs can be discovered and understood through historical research.

No serious historical methodology can proceed without critically examining the concepts it is putting into play, and few terms in contemporary discourse are more contested than *nature* and *Indians*.

"The idea nature," Raymond Williams has written, "contains, though often unnoticed, an extraordinary amount of human history."[2] Nature, Williams emphasizes, is an idea that shifts and changes over time. What we choose to call nature is culturally and historically specific. You can touch deer, elk, or rocks, but you cannot touch nature. It is not a timeless concept floating through history. We cannot begin our search for what various Indian groups thought about nature without leaving open the possibility that they did not think about *nature* at all. Certainly, they thought about deer, rain, fog, water, corn, camas roots, and all kinds of other nonhuman objects, but they did not necessarily group them together in the category *nature*. Various Indian peoples certainly might have had equivalent concepts, but if they did, it is the historian's job to demonstrate that they did.

There is a corollary involved in leaving our terms open to inquiry; asking questions reveals that in actual practice our methods do not stand totally separate from our findings. In fact, they constantly inform each other. The framing of our questions and our methodology proceeds in conversation with our research itself.

The second term at issue here, *Indian*, is a good example of this conversation between methods and findings. Much of the older literature proceeded on the supposition that there was a rather unproblematic racial identity and common outlook attached to the word *Indian*. The very concept *Indian* went uninterrogated, and this approach has by now been so roundly attacked that I will not proceed to recount the arguments here.[3]

But if the term *Indian* has been problematized, much popular and indeed much academic history still proceeds on the assumption that there was a coherent "Indian" attitude toward *nature*. J. Donald Hughes writes that "when one asks a traditional Indian, 'How much of the earth is sacred space?' the answer is unhesitating: 'All.'" As an illustration, he cites Chief Seattle.[4] The easy methodological attack on Hughes is his failure to question a source, the supposed speech of Chief Seattle, that is almost certainly a fabrication.[5] But I think the more crucial issue is the easy acceptance of the term *traditional Indian* with all its universalizing tendencies. Having accepted the idea of this pan-tribal traditional Indian, one misses all the specific false notes in Seattle's speech and hears only its resonance with our construction: the traditional Indian. We cannot move from specific studies to universal Indian beliefs. Richard Nelson, for example, although he makes methodological mistakes of his own, carefully emphasizes that he is looking at Koyukon attitudes toward nature in *Make Prayers to the Raven*. Koyukon beliefs cannot stand for the beliefs of all Native Americans regarding the natural environment.[6]

This tendency to universalize and essentialize *Indian* can take quite specific environmental forms. Indians can be constructed, for instance, as the antithesis of history, which, in turn, is constructed as the antithesis of nature. Since a historical methodology presumes a history to study, defining Indians as outside history as we understand it creates a few problems. But according to Calvin Martin, *Indian* supposedly "subscribed to a philosophy of history, and of time, profoundly different from ours."[7] Our history, according to Martin, ignores the "biological perspective" of Indian history.[8]

Indians look not for history but for the "timeless wisdom of the human species, 'the phylogenetic content of human experience.'"[9] Historians, Martin contends, "need to get out of history, as we know it, if we wish to write authentic histories of American Indians."[10] Historical methodology, I will be the first to admit, is of very little use if one is attempting to get out of history.[11]

I accept none of Martin's arguments or premises, but my point here is not to argue with him but, rather, to turn him to a methodological purpose. Martin's attack on history is, in fact, itself a history, and shows the difficulties of using history to escape history. He gives a history of the invention of history.[12] Martin finds himself relying on history itself to discredit historical consciousness.[13]

But beyond this, Martin's history shows how not to frame historical questions. Martin phrases his question in such a way that there can be only one answer. Martin asserts that "real Indians" do not think in linear time, never have and never will. This statement demands a history, for how could we know this is true unless we go back and examine conceptions of time among various Indian groups in the past? The question would be: Are there Indian peoples who think in terms of linear time and conceive of a linear history? For this to be an operational question, there has to be the possibility of more than one answer. But Martin structures his argument as a tautology, for his definition of an Indian is, in effect, a person descended from the original inhabitants of the Americas who does not recognize linear time. Any Indian contaminated with linear thinking is no longer a "real" Indian.[14]

This tactic does not place Indians outside history; it places Martin outside usual historical practice. Unless a statement is posed so that it is refutable, it is not a meaningful historical question.[15]

The first step of any historical methodology, then, is asking operational questions. Let me drive this home with one final example of a bad question: Were Indians environmentalists?

To show why this is a bad question, I'll tell you a story about a seven year old, the son of a friend of my wife. The seven year old is Puyallup; he listens to adults talk about how whites have changed Puget Sound. He thinks about it and what the world must have been like before whites came. Old ways have changed; things once permitted have been curtailed. Before whites came, he decided in the way seven year olds decide such things, Indians did not have to drive on the right side of the road. They could drive their cars wherever they pleased.

But asking if Indians could drive on the wrong side of the road before whites came is not much different from asking if Indians were environmentalists. Both assume that a current set of ideas and practices can be read back into the past. A seven year old assumes there were cars, roads, drivers; those who ask if Indians were environmentalists assume there was a "nature" that corresponds to our "nature" and practices that can be evaluated according to our definitions of environmentalism. In both cases very twentieth-century practices and concepts are read back onto the past.[16]

Posing questions is, of course, only the first step. Answering them is the trick. Since Indian peoples themselves have left us very few records, we rely largely on records produced by non-Indians and on much more recent accounts left by Indians. Now given a certain construction of Indian societies, this lack of records from the past is not really an issue. An extreme view, represented by a colleague of mine at the University of Washington, a very good ethnobotanist and anthropologist named Eugene Hunn. According to Eugene Hunn, and to paraphrase an old Who song, a good informant can see for millennia. This same practice is often asserted, at least implicitly, by the description of certain practices or beliefs as traditional. In one form this embrace of tradition is straightforward and regards the past as transparent.[17]

This embracing of an unchanging tradition is, however, so extreme that it virtually negates history itself. It brackets off part of a culture so as to make it immune from the changes affecting everything around it. We have now a considerable literature on the syncretic nature of many "traditional" Indian beliefs. Sam Gill's *Mother Earth* might be controversial, but it does show the necessity of recognizing the long time that whites and Indians have been in contact and in conversation. There are numerous outside influences on modern Indian beliefs and abundant evidence that they change over time.[18]

Much more common is a second methodological technique: upstreaming, which is connected with the work of William Fenton. Upstreaming starts from a plausible premise. Current cultural formulations about things such as nature have not been formed from whole cloth. Basic cultural patterns remain constant over long periods of time. They have a history. Therefore we can, in effect, disaggregate current customs, beliefs, and practices and look for replicas in the past. So far so good. When reliable sources at both ends of the time span describe similar practices, we can supposedly use safely more abundant modern information to fill in what we do not know about ancient beliefs and practice.[19]

There are two problems here. First, it assumes that the social group in question (the tribe, or nation) has remained relatively constant. Second, it assumes that if rituals or practices exist across time then the meaning and significance of these practices also exists relatively unchanged across time. Both are problematic.

We cannot assume obvious connections between modern Indian groups and historic groups bearing the same names. Historians have sometimes presumed that any Indian group and its cultural practices could potentially be traced back to an ancestral group living before European contact. Recent work, however, has convincingly demonstrated that many tribes are very much historic creations. They did not exist before contact and more than the modern category *Americans* existed before contact. James Merrell's work on the Catawbas and J. Leitch Wright's history of the Muscogolees are two prominent examples.[20]

But the main problem with upstreaming is that similar words, customs, and practices can hold radically different meanings at various points in time. There is much, for example, that is constant in a Catholic mass, but few historians would argue that we could therefore take the beliefs of modern Catholicism and fix them on medieval Catholicism. We do not attempt to do so because we have abundant sources on medieval Catholicism that both show us that this is not true and make it unnecessary to do so. We, however, lack such sources for many Indian peoples, and so upstreaming has considerable appeal. We would be wise to resist the temptation as much as possible.

I think the basic technique in reconstructing older worlds has to remain very close to traditional historical practice: close reading, evaluation, and contextualization of the records. Our basic rule is to know what they are, why they were produced, when they were produced, and what they represent.

Much of what we then do is a kind of literary analysis, but with a difference. History is an act of interpretation; it is, among other things, a reading and re-reading of documents.[21] Ideally, our methods are always comparative. We compare documents; we read them against each other. We order them chronologically. Deconstruction is, in a sense, what historians have done for a considerable time. We look for assumptions; hidden threads of connections, we probe for absences.

But in Indian history at the earliest stages we are dealing with an imperial history whose documents are not produced by Indians and which both record the reduction of Indians to a European order and understanding and are one of the means of their reduction. Those documents rarely contain Indian writing, but they often contain Indian voices, or what purport to be Indian voices. We need, of course, to be sure that voices speaking are, in fact, Indian. Whites often speak through Indians, particularly when Indians speak of nature. From the Adario of the Baron de Lahotan to Seattle's speech, to modern books like the *Daughters of Copper Woman*, we have had a whole array of fake Indian voices as well as the mixed Indian/white voice of classic accounts such as Black Elk.[22]

The lack of "Indian" sources might seem on first glance a debilitating liability, but it can in certain circumstances be a singular advantage. Many of the Indian voices that survive in the earliest and most problematic documents are talking to outsiders in circumstances in which both they and their listeners needed to reach a common understanding. They are engaged in a language that creates what I have elsewhere described as the middle ground.

A large chunk of our early documents, then, are conversations between people who do not completely understand each other. Methodologically this has implications. "To know a culture," Greg Deming has written, "is to know its system of expressed meanings. To know cultures in contact is to know the misreadings of meaning." We are connoisseurs of misreadings. We rarely know Indians alone; we always know them in conversation with whites. During early contact situations we never get transparent accounts that allow us to peer into a world of Indian meanings. We get mutual misreadings which often become a new common reading: a middle ground.[23]

My own operating assumption is that we will never recover a pure Indian past, a purely Indian view of the natural world as it existed before whites, because we are prisoners of the documents. What we have is mixture, impurity, and dirtiness. To seek purity is to create falsity. In Greg Deming's metaphor, this kind of ethnohistorical construction is a history of beaches. We know little of the islands that lie beyond.[24]

But to be trapped on the beach does not mean that we might not at least look into the interior. We have limited lines of sight into the islands. We have what archaeology gives us, but archaeology's ability to recreate worlds of meaning is very limited. A second line of sight comes through language. A third comes through what we might call spatial histories.

Historians have done very little with language because so few historians know any native languages. Our argument has been that there are no, or very few, documents in the language and very often no or very few native speakers are left, so what is the point of learning it? To this, we quite legitimately add a third objection: languages change like everything else. The language recorded at a given point is not necessarily the historical language.

All that is true, but languages usually change relatively slowly. Preserved in the language are conceptual frameworks, categorizations of the world that structure how a speaker perceives and organizes the world. In them are potential insights into worlds we do not know, but to follow them we need linguistic skills that most historians do not possess.

The Lushootseed language of southern Puget Sound, for instance, is now nearly extinct, but in it are clues to a way of viewing and understanding the world. There are native words that serve as straight equivalents for English words, words for porpoise, various varieties of salmon, bullheads, candlefish, and so on, but more revealing are words without direct equivalents. There are words for old salmon that has already spawned and is about to die and what fish in general are called after spawning.[25] There are classifications such as *tataculbix*—large animals—which refer not only to size but to use: large animals are food for the people.[26]

Language connects with a second way of recovering an Indian view of the world that moves behind the documents. Spatial history concerns the movement of people across the land. Metaphorically, Europeans remained on beaches, but in actuality they moved inland. Their records of travel become sources for a spatial history which is not a history of what they discovered, what they believed was already constituted, but instead a history of their movements themselves, of why they went where they did, of how and why they created boundaries. They turned space into place. They constituted a world and as they did so they often revealed another world, another possible organization of space that they were in the process of either destroying or covering over. Where they found Indians, where Indians sought to block their path or steer them, the places Indians had named and occupied before them all emerge in their travelings and can become the stuff of a spatial history critical to environmental history, which always has to be located in space.

Court cases filed by the Hopi and Zuni have provided abundant materials for spatial histories, but as an example of different conceptions of the world that can be partially retrieved let me again turn to Lushootseed. There was in the late nineteenth century a long battle over the name of Mount Rainier. Seattle wanted Mount Rainier; Tacoma wanted, not surprisingly, Tacoma, which was derived from the Lushootseed $teq^wube?$. $Teq^wube?$ is usually translated as "permanently snow covered mountain,"[27] and it refers actually to all mountains that have this character. Mount Rainier was just the supreme exemplar of a type. But the derivation of the name seems to come from words meaning literally "mountain bearing water." But what does it mean to be a mountain bearing water? A source of rivers? Glaciers? There seems to be a spatial relation here, a history, which sets the landscape in motion. Around such questions can come recovery over an older categorization of the world.

We do not have such histories yet. Paul Carter's *Road to Botany Bay* is the beginning of such spatial history in Australia, although he questions whether creating a European spatial history can simultaneously reveal outlines of a native one. What we have here in the works of scholars who have paid attention to Indian movements, boundaries, and names upon the land is an indication of the ways in which such a spatial history might be written. Bill Cronon, in *Changes in the Land*;[28] Eugene Hunn, in *Nch'i-wana*; Richard Hart, in the work he has done for Hopi and Zuni court cases; all indicate the possibilities of such projects.[29]

II

The second Big Question—How do we know how Indians acted in the past in regard to the natural world and what the consequences of their actions were?—carries into another set of methodological dilemmas. This question involves correlating what the landscape looked like with descriptions of Indian action. Our descriptions of both actions and landscape are partial, fragmentary, and not completely reliable. Methodologically, this is actually quite comforting. It is the kind of problem historians routinely confront. But historians, in working with this material, do not work alone. Much environmental history is interdisciplinary in the sense that historians use the findings and raw data, and much less often the methods, of other disciplines. Other scholars, in turn, use the data and findings of environmental historians. They misuse our data; we misuse theirs.

Most historians recognize the fragmentary and complicated nature of evidence. We do not treat what survives from the past as if it were in any way a random or scientific sample of documents, let alone that those documents preserve some representative random slice of human behavior. Some scientists in using historical evidence, however, sometimes treat this evidence as if it were, indeed, a random sample of Indian actions. Emily Russell, an ecologist, has, for example, made an argument for a limited Indian use of fire in the sixteenth and seventeenth centuries on the basis of European accounts reporting Indian use of fire.[30] Essentially, she evaluated sources mentioning fire as if they were a sample of Indian activities. Specific mentions of Indian burning were few; therefore, Indian burning was rare. This, of course, does not follow, but it raises an interesting issue. How do we know that Indians all across the continent burned the woods or grasslands regularly if this is not something we can easily demonstrate from the records alone?

To make the case, historians borrow from ecological studies and risk misusing ecologist's sources just as they sometimes misuse ours. We want to determine, if possible, what a landscape that was burned regularly might look like and, if it is possible to determine, whether natural fires alone might produce such a landscape. If, in fact, we find that the landscape described at contact gives signs of regular burning, and we can determine the approximate rate at which natural fires occur, and we have accounts of Indian-set fires, then we can begin to make better claims for Indian actions. If, for example, natural fires are rare but we have accounts of vegetation that thrives in frequently burned landscapes and we have even scattered accounts of Indian burning, then we can suggest that we are seeing a pyrogenic landscape.[31]

There is a second technique. If we can determine when Indian-set fires were eliminated and trace the results of this fire suppression, then we can reason that at least part of the earlier landscape may very well have been the result of Indian burning. To do this, historians need to use specialized studies that include examination of fire scarring, dendrochronology, and repeat photography. All of these methods appear in the literature. We are methodological parasites. Our conclusions depend on feeding off the work of others.[32]

There is a danger involved in this kind of parasitism and historians have already encountered it. We become prisoners of the conceptual framework of those outside our discipline and when their work changes or falls apart, so does ours. A crisis in ecology has had profound effects on environmental history. I will use myself as an example.

In 1980 I published a revised version of my doctoral dissertation with a rather turgid title that I have never been allowed to live down: *Land Use, Environment and Social Change: The Shaping of Island County, Washington*. The early chapters concern the landscape Indian peoples created in Island County and how it changed with white settlement. In the book, I used ecological concepts like community, succession, climax, and ecosystem unproblematically, as if they were scientific descriptions of actual things or events in nature. I did this even though within the discipline of ecology, these ideas had already come under attack. Looking back now, I realize that this book and other historical studies were themselves undermining such ecological concepts even as they relied on them. Historians were describing a human impact upon the natural world—including an Indian impact—so pervasive that it made questions of climax and successions seem abstractions with few equivalents in the actual landscape. The very scope of the changes that I described in the book should have made me more suspicious of what I mistook for unquestioned orthodoxy. Like most scholars, however, I was more polite and less belligerent when intruding upon disciplines other than my own.

Any intersection of the methods of different disciplines is fraught with danger. But there are also considerable opportunities. Historical studies have had a significant impact on ecological studies. Ecologists who once assumed little or limited human impact on environments before the introduction of European agriculture now are much more aware of a wide range of Indian activities from burning to grazing of domestic livestock, to farming. But at the same time the insistence of historians on these activities has undermined their own easy reliance on a methodology borrowed from an old and now obsolete ecology, and has forced them to pay more attention to newer ecological constructions in which stability plays little part and contingency is as prevalent as in history. Historians have to be aware of such changes. Historians of Indian peoples are not ecologists, but ecological studies become one of our major sources in reconstructing Indian actions.

This essay is not intended to be a mere listing of ways that historians reconstruct landscapes and surmise Indian actions, but instead to stress that the techniques for recovering these landscapes, which include dendrochronology, pollen studies, repeat photography, GIS mapping, and numerous techniques that are being developed almost constantly, become a critical part of the methodological tool kit.

This methodological tool kit is inherently unstable. Developing a historical methodology, particularly in an interdisciplinary field, means constant attention to what you are doing and what those in the fields you plunder are doing. Not only do your own findings, and those of your colleagues, influence your methods, but the basic concepts that underlie methods you borrow from other fields can be about as stable as California. Intellectual earthquakes, fires, storms, and landslides can send structures you think secure tumbling down. If interdisciplinary history is not going to be one field borrowing the mistakes of another, we need to be constantly aware of other disciplines. What seems certain is that the methodologies we learn in graduate school will not be the methodologies at the end of our own practice as historians.

Notes

1. I should add that I have chosen the easy questions for this methodological enterprise, for these two questions are linked to two much harder ones, namely:

How do we know what the natural world Indians acted upon actually looked like?

How do we know the relationship between how Indians changed the natural world and the changes in their own society? Summarized, all these questions amount to: What did they think, what did they do, where did they do it, and what happened as a result?

2. Raymond Williams, "Ideas of Nature," in his *Problems in Materialism and Culture* (London, 1980), 67.

3. Robert Berkhofer, Jr., *The White Man's Indian: Images of the American Indian from Columbus to Present* (New York, 1978).

4. J. Donald Hughes and Jim Swan, "How Much of the Earth Is Sacred Space?" *Environmental Review* 10 (1986), 247.

5. Rudolf Kaiser, "Chief Seattle's Speeche(es): American Origins and European Reception," in Brian Swann and Arnold Krupat, eds., *Recovering the Word: Essays on Native American Literature* (Berkeley, 1987), 497–537.

6. Richard Nelson, *Make Prayers to the Raven* (Chicago, 1986), xvi.

7. Calvin Martin, *The American Indian and the Problem of History* (New York, 1987), 6.

8. Ibid., 8.

9. Ibid., 20.

10. Ibid., 15.

11. Martin has reiterated and further developed these ideas in a second book: Calvin Martin, *In the Spirit of the Earth: Rethinking History and Time* (Baltimore: Johns Hopkins, 1992). Truth for Martin is best revealed in the paleolithic, but it is transcendent. We supposedly need to recover a primal consciousness and lose our historical consciousness. History is a curse we are trying to escape. See, for example, Martin, *In the Spirit of the Earth*, 118–24. As Martin recognizes, his own argument is very close to the much older construction of Indians as noble savages who give us a window onto universal human beginnings and into human nature.

12. It is not only a history, it is an academic history complete with footnotes. His sources are sources that represent a past located precisely in time and connected to our own. *Spirit of the Earth* cites Indian views by referring to historical documents and academic monographs; for example, Marc Lecarbot, *The History of New France* . . . (Paris, 1609; 3d ed., 1618); Marshall Sahlins, *Islands of History* (Chicago, 1985).

13. Martin, *In the Spirit of the Earth*, 122.

14. See Martin's contrast between Navajos who are "part of it" and those who are not, in ibid., 23, 24.

15. Martin's methodological failing here is more common than we might think. We see a milder version of it in Richard Nelson's *Make Prayers to the Raven*. Nelson writes in his introduction that he has "made a personal choice against discussing the negative elements and the malefactors, which of course exist in every culture." Nelson's version of real Koyukons are those who do not transgress Koyukon values, which is, of course, to read out of Koyukon society actual Koyukons who did not share or observe Koyukon values or whom Nelson perceives as negative. We know real Koyukon values and practices because those who do not observe them are not real Koyukons. This is the equivalent of arguing that all real Americans are law abiding because those who violate the laws are not real Americans.

16. I am not saying the issue under consideration is trivial. I am only arguing that a good methodology demands better questions. Did Indians influence later white conservationists or environmentalists? Did environmentalists seek to equate their ideas with those of Indians? Did Indians seek to equate some of their ideas with environmentalism and become environmentalists themselves? *These* are operational questions. See George L. Cornell, "Native American Contributions to the Formation of the Contemporary Conservation Ethic" (Ph.D. diss., Michigan State University, 1982).

17. Eugene Hunn with James Selam and family, Nch'i-wana, "The Big River": Mid Columbia Indians and Their Land (Seattle, 1990).

18. Sam D. Gill, *Mother Earth* (Chicago, 1987).

19. James Axtell gives a concise definition of upstreaming, in his "Ethnohistory: A Historian's Viewpoint," in James Axtell, *The European and the Indian: Essays in the Ethnohistory of Colonial North America* (New York, 1981), 9–10.

20. James Merrell, *The Indians' New World: Catawbas and Their Neighbors from European Contact through the Era of Removal* (Chapel Hill, 1989); J. Leitch Wright, Jr., *Creeks and Seminoles: The Destruction and Regeneration of the Muscolgulge People* (Lincoln, 1986).

21. For an interesting discussion of this and its implications, see Paul Carter, *The Road to Botany Bay* (Chicago, 1987), 325–26.

22. For Seattle, see Kaiser, "Chief Seattle's Speeche(es)," in Swann and Krupat, *Recovering the Word*, 497–537. For Black Elk, see Raymond J. De Mallie, ed., *The Sixth Grandfather: Black Elk's Teachings Given to John G. Neihardt* (Lincoln, 1984), 1–99. The Snoqualmie tribe, among others, treats the speech as genuine; see Snoqualmie Falls Brochure, Snoqualmie Tribe, Redmond, Washington.

23. Greg Deming, *Islands and Beaches: Discourse on a Silent Land: Marquesas 1774–1880* (Chicago, 1980), 6.

24. I have borrowed this metaphor from Greg Deming, *Islands and Beaches*. Richard White, *The Middle Ground: Indians Empires, and Republics in the Great Lakes Region, 1650–1815* (New York, 1991), x. See also Eric Wolf, *Europe and the Peoples without History* (Berkeley, 1982).

This problem of fragmentary records produced largely by non-Indians begins to fade as we reach the late nineteenth and early twentieth centuries, but these accounts too, I would argue, must be read as conversations. Even when Indians speak, they are addressing whites or speaking at the instigation of whites. Their views are still best regarded as parts of conversations rather than as accounts of some isolate and pristine world. An easy example would be the writings of Charles Eastman; see, for example, Charles Eastman, *The Soul of the Indian: An Interpretation* (1911; repr., Lincoln, 1980).

25. Dawn Bates, Thom Hess, and Vi Hilbert, *Lushootseed Dictionary* (Seattle, 1994), 312 (see listings under *fish*).

26. Ibid., 219.

27. Ibid., 332.

28. Cronon, *Changes in the Land: Indians, Colonists, and the Ecology of New England* (New York, 1983).

29. Hunn, *Nch'i-wana*; E. Richard Hart, ed., *Zuni and the Courts: A Struggle for Sovereign Land Rights* (Lawrence, Kans., 1995).

30. Emily W. B. Russell, "Indian-Set Fires in the Forests of the Northeastern United States," *Ecology* (1983), 78–88.

31. See Stephen Pyne, *Fire in America: A Cultural History of Wildland and Rural Fire* (Princeton, N.J., 1982).

32. George E. Gruell, "Fire and Vegetative Trends in the Northern Rockies: Interpretations from 1871–1982 Photographs," USDA, Forest Service, Intermountain Forest and Range Experiment Station, Ogden, Utah 84401, *General Technical Report, INT-158*, December 1983; George Gruell, "Indian Fires in the Interior West: A Widespread Influence," *Wilderness Fire Symposium*, Missoula, Mont., Nov. 15–18, 1983; Stephen F. Arno and George E. Gruell, "Fire History at the Forest Grassland Ecotone in Southwestern Montana," *Journal of Range Management* 36 (1983), 332–36; Stephen F. Arno, "Ecological Effects and Management Implications of Indian Fires," *Wilderness Fire Symposium*, Missoula, Mont., Nov. 15–18, 1983; Stephen W. Barrett and Stephen F. Arno, "Indian Fires as an Ecological Influence in the Northern Rockies," *Journal of Forestry* (October 1982), 647–50.

6
Power of the Spoken Word
Native Oral Traditions in American Indian History

Angela Cavender Wilson

Since its inception, the area of American Indian history has been dominated by non-Indian historians who use non-Indian sources to create non-Indian interpretations about American Indians and their pasts. These historians have rarely bothered to ask, or even seem to care, what the Indians they are studying might have to say about their work. Very few have attempted to find out how native people would interpret, analyze, and question the written documents they confront, nor have they asked if the native people they are studying have their own versions or stories of their past that might be pertinent to their analysis. As long as history continues to be studied and written in this manner, the field should more appropriately be called non-Indian perceptions of American Indian history.

To truly gain a grasp of the field of American Indian history, native sources must be consulted. Because few native people have left written records for historians to ponder, most of these native sources will be our family and tribal historians relaying oral history. The majority of academic historians thus far have ignored our spokespeople and attempted to write in the field with only a portion of the information, only a portion of the available sources. If an archive was filled somewhere with relevant information to a scholar's study and s/he chose to ignore it, accusations of sloppy scholarship would be hurled from all directions. But if a scholar in the field of American Indian history ignores the vast amount of oral sources, the scholar's integrity is preserved through the use of this time period," or "fact cannot be distinguished from fancy," or "I don't know any Indians!"

Would scholars in the field of history today attempt to write a history of Germany without consulting any German sources? Would a scholar of Chinese history attempt to write Chinese history without consulting Chinese sources? Is it simply because most of our sources are oral rather than written, because we have put our faith in our elders rather than on paper, that this double standard is tolerated? It seems ridiculous that questions so basic even have to be asked about work done in American Indian history.

Moreover, there is an accompanying problem with the collection of oral accounts, and that is the issue of language. Would the scholar of German history not bother to learn to speak German? Or would the scholar of Chinese history not bother to learn Chinese? Recently, while reading a book on the Nahuas of Mexico by James Lockhart, I was struck by the following statement, "The gods of the disciplines seemed to have decreed that historians should study Indians indirectly, leaving it to others, mainly anthropologists, to approach them through their own language."[1] Some might claim that the diversity of native peoples precludes the study of specific languages, but again I would ask does one specializing in European history not bother to study or develop a working knowledge of any of the languages of the European groups? Hardly; in fact, the tendency would be to become at least familiar, if not fluent in several languages.

If these are contemporary flaws in the way American Indian history is written, how should one attempt to approach the subject? This is the topic I wish to address because I see the incorporation and use of oral history, regardless of one's area of specialty, as not merely that of another source, but as the greatest resource upon which the discipline of American Indian history will proceed. However, it is also the area that is the most difficult to engage in, interpret, and incorporate into standard texts, because for non-Indians it means attempting to understand a completely foreign worldview which does not easily conform to Western standards of historical analysis and writing. As a result, there are important moral and ethical considerations that need to be addressed in terms of methodology as scholars begin to understand the power of the spoken word and to incorporate native oral traditions into American history. These issues will be the focus of this essay.

Before I begin, I must clarify the terms *oral history* and *oral tradition* as I will be using them because my definitions differ from those used and accepted in the field. David Henige, in his book *Oral Historiography*, differentiates between oral history and oral tradition when he says, "As normally used nowadays, 'oral history' refers to the study of the recent past by means of life histories or personal recollections, where informants speak about their own experiences . . . oral tradition should be handed down for at least a few generations."[2] Jan Vansina has a similar definition for oral history but further breaks the area into categories, and he differs with Henige in the definition of oral tradition only by excluding the need for a collective memory. He says, "The sources of oral historians are reminiscences, hearsay, or eyewitness accounts about events and situations which are contemporary, that is, which occurred during the lifetime of the informants. This differs from the oral traditions in that oral traditions are no longer contemporary. They have passed from mouth to mouth, for a period beyond the lifetime of the informants."[3]

These definitions are applicable to Native American oral history and oral tradition only in a very limited way. Native peoples' life histories, for example, often incorporate the experiences of other both human and nonhuman beings, as well as the experiences of their ancestors. In addition, by suggesting that people living today are outside an oral tradition, these definitions assume the contemporary person would not interpret the tradition as new materials are incorporated into the understanding of the past, thereby implying a kind of static and tradition-bound nature.

From a native perspective, I would suggest instead that the definition of oral history is contained within that of the oral tradition. For the Dakota, "oral tradition" refers to the way in which information is passed on rather than the length of time something has been told. Hence, personal experiences, pieces of information, events, incidents, and other phenomena can become a part of the oral tradition at the moment they happen or at the moment they are told, as long as the person adopting the memory is part of an oral tradition. This definition also implies that while those belonging to an oral tradition would be able to relate aspects of oral history, not everyone relating oral history necessarily belongs to an oral tradition.

So who does belongs to an oral tradition? Charles Eastman, a Wahpetonwan Dakota, reveals in his autobiography, *Indian Boyhood*, the distinct way in which oral skill in our culture was developed:

> Very early, the Indian boy assumed the task of preserving and transmitting the legends of his ancestors and his race. Almost every evening a myth, or a true story of some deed done in the past, was narrated by one of the parents or grandparents, while the boy listened with parted lips and glistening eyes. On the following evening, he was usually required to repeat it. If he was not an apt scholar, he struggled long with his task; but as a rule, the Indian boy is a good listener and has a good memory, so that his stories were tolerably well mastered. The household became his audience, by which he was alternately criticized and applauded.[4]

This excerpt highlights the rigorous and extensive training required of young boys, as Eastman is speaking of his own upbringing, but would certainly be applicable to the training of girls also. Hence the Dakota definitions of oral tradition is based on the assumption that the ability to remember is an acquired skill—one that is acutely developed or neglected. Eastman also describes the differentiation between myth and true stories, necessitating an understanding of history as being encompassed in oral tradition.

While oral accounts collected from all native people may be valuable if those people are speaking from a position of authority about their own life experiences, not all native people currently belong to an oral tradition. Therefore, this essay will not attempt to address methodology in oral history as it applies to all native people, but specifically those belonging to an oral tradition, which often means working with the elders of our societies. These will also most often be the people who are carriers of our other traditions as well, such as language, ceremonies, and customs—a fact that has a number of implications.

When people first suggest an interest in the collection of oral data from native societies a number of questions run through my mind—questions such as: What are the motives behind this desire? How will the information be used? In what kind of context? Does the individual know the culture they hope to extract information from well enough? And, perhaps most importantly, who will benefit from its documentation? These are all questions that should be dealt with in an honest manner before anyone even considers beginning a project, because I know if these questions run through my mind they will most likely be running through the minds of other native people as well. Dealing with these questions, then, will be the first step in acknowledging the ethics involved in working with live subjects who are capable of speaking for themselves, and engaging in a process loaded with moral considerations.

I raise these questions because I do not believe this is something everyone who wants to could or should do. There exists a kind of arrogance in the fields of history and anthropology based on an assumption that scholars in these disciplines have a right to information and source materials, even when dealing with live people. Furthermore, the belief is that once stories are documented, scholars have a right to do with them whatever they wish.[5] However, no such rights are guaranteed simply because one has a Ph.D. In fact, those letters after the name mean very little in most native communities.

The collection of stories from the oral tradition is not a project that should be engaged in lightly. Language and interpretation remain huge stumbling blocks for those outside a culture, and can be problems for even those within a culture. Many elders from coast to coast speak their own languages, and even those who are bilingual may be much more comfortable and eloquent when speaking in their native tongue. Out of respect for them and the cultures they are a part of, as well as for a greater understanding of the worldview from which they come, I would suggest learning the language before at-tempting to work with the stories from within that tradition. This in itself suggests a lengthy, if not a lifetime, commitment, and certainly not some-thing that can be accomplished with six months of funding from a research grant. The importance of language and linguistic studies to the collection of oral data has been recognized by oral historians working with African groups is particular, but seems to be an issue avoided by historians in the United States and in Canada.[6]

A number of universities currently have native language programs, which can be a starting point for some, but in most instances, and always eventu-ally, it means becoming involved with native people, befriending them, and placing oneself in a position of vulnerability (not interacting with Indians as an authority or expert on their history and culture, but as a student of theirs). Not only will those taking this route learn a great deal about the culture they are dealing with, but such interaction would also provide the opportu-nity to build connections with those who will mostly likely be the most knowledgeable about the culture—the fluent speakers of the language!

Sustained interaction with a culture different from one's own should ide-ally also produce a sense of some of the basic concepts that seem to be com-mon to most native groups, such as the importance of community and the notion of reciprocity. As close relationships are developed with native people, even those from outside cultures are made a part of the community and oftentimes are even adopted into specific families, and while many privi-leges come from such relationships there are also as many responsibilities. One has only to glance through many of the "as-told-to autobiographies" of native people written throughout this century, primarily by anthropologists, to get a glimpse of what happens when non-native people do not realize their responsibilities to the people and cultures with whom they have worked. Many of the Indian people who adopted these scholars as children, grand-children, or siblings would probably be horrified if they knew how their "kin" had used their stories and their culture.[7]

In addition, familiarity with the concept of reciprocity breeds a realiza-tion of the need to give something back to both the individual and the cul-ture from whom and from which one has taken material. This goes far beyond the economic compensation that many scholars have used in exchange for their "informants'" time. Rather, what is called for is an acknowledgment of a moral responsibility to give back in a far more profound way, one that matches the value of the stories that are shared. Indeed, as a Dakota I would carry that a step further because I come from a culture in which generosity, one of our cardinal virtues, is stressed far more than reciprocity, meaning that there is a need to give even more than what one received. In light of this, a central consideration would have to be whether such work will help or possibly hurt a community by demeaning or discrediting its elders or culture.

This is where the question of who will benefit from the documentation of these stories comes into play. Imagine sitting before a room full of elders from the culture you are studying, after your first book on them has been published, and having to be accountable for your methodology, your translations, your editing, your terminology, your analysis and interpretation, and how you have used their stories. If this does not make you sweat, it should, because while a situation as programmed as this may never occur, the time for accountability of the work of historians and anthropologists has definitely come. Ramon Gutierrez's work on the Pueblo peoples is testimony to this.[8]

Once a familiarity with the language and culture of a native group has been established, I have several suggestions for scholars committed to following indigenous protocol. First, an acknowledgment and understanding of the internal mechanisms native people have for determining within their own communities whether they have information relevant to a scholar's study must be made; then, the community must decide who, in their society, is authorized and informed enough to share information; what information is appropriate to share must be decided upon; and lastly, communities must decide whether they feel a scholar is respectful enough of their culture to merit their trust in sharing valuable insights. Some of these issues have been suggested by other scholars in the area of oral history. For instance, Vansina argues, "it is important to note who the author of the recorded version was. If he was a professional, did his performance belong to genre reserved to professionals? Was he entitled to perform or not?"[9] However, even while making these distinctions, the ethical issues involved are largely ignored by these scholars in favor of issues of credibility and accuracy.

An understanding of these internal mechanisms and answers to the questions posed above may be gained through such informal means as asking around in a community who the elders are who might have information to share, or it might require such formalities as appearing before a tribal council to give a formal presentation on research intentions, something a graduate student I know recently had to do with the Cattaraugus Seneca Nation. If formal means are required, it is imperative that a scholar obtain this approval before continuing any further. As more and more native communities regain a sense of intellectual control over information dispersed to people outside their culture, more and more organized bodies of tribal leadership may codify a procedure for others to either access or not access this information.

Respect of limitations must also be observed. A Winnebago friend of mine who has taken Winnebago language classes in a couple of different settings has stated that the Wisconsin Winnebago have taken an active role in limiting language studies to Winnebago people. So while a non-Indian scholar may be able to utilize written linguistic sources available if s/he is precluded from working with live people, it should not be done if this goes against the wishes of the community, ethically speaking. A lack of language skills would certainly hinder a scholar's access to many of the most knowledgeable elders, and this should be considered before one decides, for example, to do Winnebago oral history.

Once mutually satisfactory arrangements about the subject of study are agreed upon, culturally appropriate protocol should be observed. In some native communities this may mean offering tobacco to an elder, it may mean providing gifts of food or money, or it may mean asking for their help in a specific way. Until the appropriate process for collection of data is determined, no attempt should be made to collect oral accounts. Understanding and respecting this protocol will ensure that the relationship between the scholar and the native person with whom they are working will be off to a good start.

The process of recording stories may then begin. Native people have varying concerns about how stories should be written down, or whether they should be written at all, whether their native language should be used, whether video or audio equipment should be used, what time of day or season of the year the stories should be told, and where the native person is most comfortable telling the stories. All involved parties should discuss these issues and decisions should be made about them in advance of any recording. Wishes of the native person should be honored in all instances. Videotaping, with backup audio recordings, is ideal, in my opinion, because the gestures and facial expressions are preserved this way and may greatly enhance interpretations in the translation process. In addition, as mentioned earlier, it is important to record native people in the language in which they are most comfortable and eloquent. While this may put the recorder or the scholar at a disadvantage, I would rather see the scholar struggling with lack of eloquence and discomfort, rather than putting our elders in such a position.

One of the most beneficial and powerful ways a scholar can give back to a community is through the use of language. Because many native communities are grappling with the issue of language retention, bilingual texts that may be used for language study are extremely valuable. An excellent example of work of this nature is being done by John Nichols, who has dedicated a lifetime to working among the Anishinabe of Minnesota, specifically with elders Maude Kegg and Earl Nyholm. Together, Nichols and Kegg have produced a number of source materials based on the oral accounts told to Nichols by Kegg. Their works represent truly collaborative projects, in which the native voice is not overpowered by that of the scholar, and which will contribute a great deal to the furtherance of Ojibwe language. The stories were originally told in the Ojibwe language and then transcribed, which Kegg and Nichols then worked together to translate. In addition to these bilingual texts, Nichols and Nyholm have recently produced together the second edition of *A Concise Dictionary of Minnesota Ojibwe*, which shows a great deal of tenacity and commitment.[10] Because processes like this are painfully slow and tedious, particularly for those learning about a culture foreign to them, it means spending an unusually long time in the research process and becoming comfortable with the idea that publications may only result after years of work.

As the historian begins to consider what aspects of stories may be of historical value, s/he is once again treading on culturally sensitive turf. After growing up in a family with a rich oral tradition and deciding to spend my life working with that tradition, I have come to realize that while I have a clear sense of the difference between myth and true stories according to my culture's standards, our oral tradition is a kind of web in which each strand is a part of the whole. The individual strands are most powerful when interconnected to make an entire web, that is, when the stories are examined in their entirety. Each of our stories possesses meaning and power, but is most significant when understood in relation to the rest of the stories in the oral tradition.

For example, while stories of "shapeshifting" are part of the Dakota reality and would belong to our categories of true stories, they make much more sense when understood in combination with some of the stories we may classify as myth—such as our Unktomi stories. Unktomi is our trickster figure who has the capacity to change form, and while Unktomi stories are told to teach and entertain they contain elements that are important in understanding our worldview as relayed in our historical stories. To get at the layers of meaning, then, I believe it is valuable for historians to become familiar with accounts outside the historical realm.

This differentiation between myths and true stories has been a source of contention between Indians and non-Indians for centuries. Non-Indians, upon hearing some of the stories, have a difficult time discerning history from myth (and many have thereby dismissed the possibility of a distinction). This is because the native relationship with the "spiritual," the "supernatural," and the "metaphysical" is not an abstract or dualistic one; the spiritual and material worlds are intimately interconnected and mutually constitutive of native "reality." This is reflected in our conception of "history." For native people, these things are perfectly "natural," "real," and "factual." Therefore, those from outside the culture would be hard pressed to prove what is myth and what is truth from the perspective of someone else's worldview.

In an essay from *The Past Meets the Present*, William Moss defines oral history and oral tradition as Henige and Vansina do, and they describe the ideal interviewing process for working with oral history, saying:

> The role of the interviewer in oral history is never entirely passive. It is always active, a dynamic interaction with the person being interviewed. The interviewer searches out memories and provokes reflections and evaluations of significance, even hypotheses that may be tested against the individual's personal experience, and challenges the respondent into further examination and reflection on assumptions and assertions made in the first instance.[11]

While Moss and other scholars may feel this is an appropriate interviewing technique for members of the communities with whom they work, I would not recommend it for working with native elders, as this type of behavior would be construed as disrespectful and aggressive. This is another example of how the tools of scholarly historical inquiry are inappropriate to cross-cultural work.

In addition to differences in worldview that become apparent in such situations, further problems arise when scholars attempt to treat oral historical material as they might deal with other written source materials. Many scholars today working with oral history recognize that oral accounts do not represent "raw data," but they nevertheless recommend using the same process of analysis as one would use for written sources. Vansina suggests that oral traditions should be treated as hypotheses, similar to a historian's hypotheses about the past, and thus should be tested as such before a scholar considers other hypotheses. He says, "To consider them first means not to accept them literally, uncritically. It means give them the attention they deserve, to take pains to prove or disprove them systematically for each case on its own merits . . . [The historian] must continue the historiological process that has been underway. This by no means is to say that the historian's interpretations should be literal. Only at the least should they be more believable than the already existing oral hypothesis."[12]

How one from outside the culture would be able to "continue the historiological process that has been underway" or how the historian decides what is a "more believable" hypothesis is beyond my comprehension. Rather, what I see happening with those specializing in the field of oral history is an attempt to make oral accounts from other cultures conform to Western notions of respectability, truth, narrative format, categories, significance, terminology, sensibility, and so forth. While I would argue that oral accounts certainly are interpretations of the past and should not be treated as raw data, I do not believe they should be tested and evaluated by Western standards, or any other standards from other cultures for that matter. The only standards that matter are those set within the culture, and if stories are still being told within the oral tradition then they have obviously passed these internal checks.

What then is the value of oral accounts and what should be done with them by historians? Bernard Fontana, more than twenty-five years ago, perceptively suggested an answer to this in his essay "American Indian Oral History: An Anthropologist's Note," stating:

> What is relevant is that someone else defines truth differently and sees history in a different way. If in collecting oral histories one aims to get the Indians' point of view, the question of veracity in our terms has little to do with it. It is veracity in their terms which counts.[13]

For a research commitment made twenty-five years ago, it is disheartening to note that little progress has been made in this direction. However, there are a few scholars making headway along these lines. More recently, David William Cohen has suggested that the rigidity in thinking about oral traditions is highly problematic, remarking about them and the cultures from which they come:

> They invite us to see individuals making and holding historical knowledge in all their complexity and individuality—considerably concerned with interests, objectives, recreation, and esteem, and rather less concerned with performing history according to some given cultural design . . . They call us to strengthen our approach to the reconstruction of the past through the reworking of our logic of the production of historical knowledge.[14]

I would suggest this challenge to "rework the logic of the production of historical knowledge" must be heeded in a drastic way, but may be most painful to historians as decisions about how accounts may be used are made. Once historians obtain stories which retain their integrity, which are considered within a larger cultural context, and which reflect a native perspective of the American Indian past, these stories can then be presented alongside other non-Indian interpretations. However, the purpose of the written sources should not be to validate, verify, or negate the native perspective. Rather, they should be used for what is significant about them culturally, internal to the culture they are from. The stories must be respected in their own right, and historians must be willing to let them stand on their own.

To elaborate on this concept, it is necessary to address the function of the oral tradition within native stories because I believe the connection native people have with their oral traditions is drastically different from how the American populace connects with their historical texts. Our stories have served and continue to serve very important functions: both the historical and mythical stories provide moral guidelines by which one should live; they teach the young and remind the old what appropriate and inappropriate behavior consists of in our cultures; they provide a sense of identity and belonging, situating community members within their lineage and establishing their relationship to the rest of the natural world; and they always serve as a source of entertainment, as well as a source of bonding and intimacy between the storyteller and the audience. These stories, much more so than the written documents by non-Indians, provide detailed descriptions about our historical players—information such as our motivations, our kinds of decision-making processes—as well as about how non-material, non-physical circumstances, or those things belonging to the unseen or spirit world, have shaped our past and our understanding of the present; and they answer many other "why" and "how" questions typically asked by the academic community. Moreover, the stories are considered by many native people to be living entities, with a power and a spirit of their own. Greg Sarris, in one of his essays on his work with Mabel McKay, relates the perspective of a Pomo woman on this subject, who tells him, "Our stories, like our lives, are living. Might as well give white man your leg or arm. No matter what he gets, he just does with it how he likes. Like our land."[15]

Consequently, ours are not merely interesting stories or a simple dissemination of historical facts, but more importantly, they are transmissions of culture upon which our survival as a people depends. In addition, I know from personal experience that as you hear the stories repeatedly through time, the stories do not remain the stories of your elders and ancestors, but your elders' and ancestors' memories become your own. Furthermore, often the stories relayed by elders contain messages that are not easily deciphered, even for those within the culture. For many, it may take years, or even a lifetime, to understand the full meaning and implications of a story heard as a child. Greg Sarris had another interesting exchange with Mabel McKay, the Pomo woman whose life story he was writing, when they had the following discussion:

> "How you going to do my book?" she asked.
> "That's what I always ask you," I shot back.
> She gave me an admonishing look. Not the answer she was looking for, I thought to myself. "I'm going to come back in the spring, like I said," I told her. "I'll finish getting the exact dates and figures that go with stories."
> She looked perplexed.
> "You know," I said, "so I can get things right. I mean your life, the story."
> She focused. "It has nothing to do with dates and that. I don't know about dates. It's everlasting what I'm talking about."[16]

Another example of a native approach to oral history may be found in the story my grandfather, Eli Taylor, tells about a spiritual figure who came among the Dakota many, many centuries ago, and as he passed on information to our people he said, "What I am telling you now, I want you to pass it on every year, from one generation to the next, from your grandchild to your great-grandchild, and your great-great-grandchild on down. Kiksuyapo (remember this)!" He said, "I will help you remember these things that I have told you." In another instance, the Dakota were told, "I will give you a strong mind to remember."[17] This story suggests that not only are our stories meant to be told orally because our tradition is of divine origin, but also that we have divine help in remembering them!

The idea, then, of someone outside the culture studying them word by word, line by line, categorizing them, scrutinizing the narrative format, dissecting their structure, analyzing their changes, and testing their credibility is at least disturbing if not downright offensive to many native people. In addition, the idea that historians could pull out the information they want and leave the rest is easily recognized as presumptuous. As I discussed these issues with other native scholars using oral history in their work, they used such phrases to describe this analysis as "robbing the stories of their context" and "sucking the life out of the stories." Certainly, this is not what our elders intend for us to do when they share the stories with us. So much of what is contained within the oral tradition may never be corroborated by any written evidence, and every inch of the continent could be excavated by archaeologists and still there may be nothing that can prove or disprove many of the stories. Because of this, it is important to note that scholars in any discipline trying to verify every story with additional evidence will quite often find themselves engaged in a futile effort. If we as native people are willing to put our stories forward with faith in our culture and elders, no further evidence is necessary—that is, if one wants to understand native perspectives of American Indian history.

One might ask how native people reconcile differing accounts, or what happens if oral sources are in direct contradiction to written sources. To respond to such questions I would like to use a concept from my own culture to explain my perspective. One of the ceremonies still practiced among my people is called in our language "hanbdeceya," or literally "crying for a vision." While this term usually makes reference to the formal ceremony in which men would go off by themselves, usually for a four-day period, fasting, praying, and singing until they received a vision, visions were given to both men and women in a number of other ways as well. An important aspect of this concept is that when one received a vision, it was not for others to question. Thus I grew up with a belief that you "respect another person's vision." This concept naturally extends to communities and cultures and seems particularly relevant to the question of what should be done with our visions of history.

This is a fundamentally different approach to others than that embraced by a Western European scholarly tradition that is largely based on Christian values and promotes a belief in only one truth, one way, one right.[18] Michael Dorris commented on this phenomena when he stated, "To admit that other, culturally divergent viewpoints are equally plausible is to cast doubt on the monolithic center of Judeo-Christian belief: that there is but one of everything—God, right way, truth—and Europeans alone knew what that was."[19] For most native people with whom I am familiar, this is not an issue.

While there might be differing stories on the same topic within any given native community, and families and individuals may differ in opinion about those stories, there is acknowledgment that there may be more than one "right" version, that stories differ according to perspective, that people's interpretations change along the way, and that some individuals may be more adept than others in relaying specific stories. This does not reduce the importance of the stories, however.

Also, my impressions are that most Indians would not expect people from other cultural traditions to discard belief systems, culture, and stories familiar to them and subscribe instead to native beliefs, culture, and stories. Instead, there is a respect among native people, especially concerning the stories, in which we can appreciate the wonderful nature of another group's stories, believe those stories, and then share ours with them, knowing we will receive the same courtesy. Personally, as a Dakota, I do not expect all non-Dakota to subscribe to our notions of truth, reality, or history. However, I would and do take to task those who disregard our cultural perspective and attempt to make what is Dakota conform to their cultural standards. Likewise, I believe many native people would object to having their stories manipulated into Western notions of history.

This hands-off approach to the analysis of American Indian oral historical accounts will be, understandably, very disturbing to academic historians. After all, what I am suggesting is that the vast majority of what has passed thus far in the field as American Indian history has not had the one component that legitimizes that title, namely, the perspective of American Indian people; and what truly is American Indian history, that is, our history as we perceive it, should be kept beyond the reach of historical analysis. These statements will be received quite uncomfortably in archives across the country and I do not mean to suggest that histories based solely on written documents are of no value. The contributions they make in understanding the written word is significant, but the limitations of their work must be acknowledged. The idea that scholars can "sift through" the biases of non–Indian written sources enough to get at the Indian perspective is presumptuous and erroneous. What I am suggesting, therefore, is that those writing history in this manner should discontinue the pretension that they are truly understanding American Indian history or that they speak for native society and perspective.

Our traditions must not be evaluated in Western terms; rather, they should be appreciated and utilized for what they do contribute to the understanding of the American Indian past. The attempt, for the most part, until now has been to continually measure native cultural characteristics against Western ideas to learn what their purpose is and what is of value in them, thus forcing native characteristics to conform to Western notions of truth instead of considering them in their own right. It is imperative that academic scholars do not take oral accounts out of their broader cultural context simply to bolster their own work and promote their own theoretical models. As native people, we have our own interpretations, sense of history, and theories, among which our stories are central. It is time that the field of history acknowledge, value, and accept as valid native concepts about our past. Only then will others begin to understand the area called American Indian history.

For those who want to commit themselves to a life of understanding American Indian peoples, the personal rewards will be great. Not only will the academic historian participate in an experiential learning process, building close relationships along the way, s/he will have a greater depth of understanding of our versions of personal and tribal histories, a sense of satisfaction in the realization of moral responsibilities, and most importantly, they will help engender scholarly works endorsed by native people and native communities. Historians and native people can work together, then, on collaborative projects in which there is mutual respect for the authority and skills that each brings to the understanding of American Indian history, and this is my hope for the future.

Notes

1. James Lockhart, *The Nahuas after the Conquest: A Social and Cultural History of the Indians of Central Mexico* (Stanford, Calif., 1992), 6.

2. David Henige, *Oral Historiography* (London, 1982), 2.

3. Jan Vansina, *Oral Tradition as History* (Madison, 1985), 12.

4. Charles Eastman, *Indian Boyhood* (1902; repr., New York, 1971), 43.

5. For an excellent discussion of an appropriate process to formalize regulations for scholars researching American Indians at the institutional level, see Devon Mihesuah, "Suggested Guidelines for Institutions with Scholars Who Conduct Research on American Indians," *American Indian Culture and Research Journal* 17:3 (1993), 131–39.

6. See Vansina, *Oral Tradition as History*, 84.

7. A dramatic example of such a violation of kinship responsibility and respect may be seen in David E. Jones, *Sanapia: Comanche Medicine Woman* (1972; repr., Prospect Heights, Ill., 1984).

8. See Ramon A. Gutierrez, *When Jesus Came the Corn Mothers Went Away: Marriage, Sexuality, and Power in New Mexico, 1500–1846* (Stanford, Calif., 1991); and *American Culture and Research Journal* 17:3 (1993), 141–77, for Pueblo commentaries on this work.

9. Vansina, *Oral Tradition as History*, 55.

10. Maude Kegg, *Portage Lake: Memories of an Ojibwe Childhood* (Edmonton, 1991); and *Oshkaabewis Native Journal* 1:2 (1990). Also, see Earl Nyholm and John Nichols, *A Concise Dictionary of Minnesota Ojibwe* (Minneapolis, 1995).

11. William Moss, "Oral History: What Is It and Where Did It Come From?" in David Stricklin and Rebecca Sharpless, eds., *The Past Meets the Present: Essays on Oral History* (Lanham, Md., 1988), 12.

12. Vansina, *Oral Tradition as History*, 196.

13. Bernard Fontana, "American Indian Oral History: An Anthropologist's Note," *History and Theory* 8:3 (1969), 370.

14. David William Cohen, "Undefining of Oral Tradition," *Ethnohistory* 36:1 (Winter 1989), 16.

15. Greg Sarris, "'What I'm Talking about When I'm Talking about My Baskets': Conversations with Mabel McKay," in Sidonie Smith and Julia Watson, eds., *De/colonizing the Subject: The Politics of Gender in Women's Autobiography* (Minneapolis, 1992), 30.

16. Greg Sarris, *Mabel McKay: Weaving the Dream* (Berkeley, 1994), 135.

17. Eli Taylor, oral history project with Angela Cavender Wilson, January 1992, not yet published.

18. *Holy Bible: The New King James Version* (Nashville, 1984), Matthew 7:6, 838.

19. Michael Dorris, "Indians on the Shelf," in Calvin Martin, ed., *The American Indian and the Problem of History* (New York, 1987), 102.

7
Methodologies in Reconstructing Native American History

Donald L. Fixico

The history of American Indians is much more complex and complicated than it is normally presumed to be. In fact, in conceptualizing the past of any Indian nation or community, it has become too simple to write American Indian history from only printed documents produced by linear-thinking white men. One must use imagination in order to consider the total picture of the history of a single Indian community or individual (such as the biography of an Indian person), and to attempt to conceive the historical reality of the person and/or his or her community.

Overall, the complexity of American Indian life and reality has been underrepresented by scholars and writers, who have produced more than thirty thousand books about Native Americans. Some scholars have written enlightening histories of American Indians, and others have raised critical questions about the general portrayal of Indian people. In attempts to alert scholars to this issue, articles have appeared in print periodically to explain the status of Indian history, or to call for a new Indian history by questioning methodologies and theories for analyzing or writing Native American history. Robert F. Berkhofer, Jr., issued a warning in 1971, in "The Political Context of a New Indian History." Much earlier, in 1957, Stanley Pargellis, in "The Problem of American Indian History," called attention to the vast diversity of Indian groups and their cultures as a problem in studying American Indian history. In the following year, 1958, James C. Olson, in "Some Reflections on Historical Method and Indian History," criticized historians for their methodology in analyzing Indian history. Jack D. Forbes followed in the next few years and, in 1963, challenged historians to be more objective in their portrayal of Native Americans, in "The Historian and the Indian: Racial Bias in American History."

Frontier historians, and historians who sometimes wrote about the frontier, included Native Americans in their Turnerian works. However, from

1968 to 1973 some of these historians began to confront the displacement of the Indian from American history. Such warnings included Jack Forbes, "Frontiers in American History and the Role of the Frontier Historian"; Richard L. Haan, "Another Example of Stereotypes on the Early American Frontier: The Imperialist Historians and the American Indian"; and Wilbur R. Jacobs, "The Indian and the Frontier in American History—A Need for Revision."

In an effort to write better American Indian history, ethnohistorians took up the cause. From 1957 to 1980 ethnohistorians calling for a change included Wilcomb E. Washburn, "A Moral History of Indian–White Relations: Needs and Opportunities for Study"; William N. Fenton, "Ethnohistory and Its Problems"; Calvin Martin, "Ethnohistory: A Better Way to Write Indian History"; and Francis Jennings, "A Growing Partnership: Historians, Anthropologists, and American Indian History." As Fenton, Martin, and Jennings cited fresh approaches in cross-cultural analysis and cross-disciplines, Patricia K. Galloway, "Ethnohistory," in Jay K. Johnson, ed., *The Development of Southeastern Archaeology* (1993), makes a valid argument that archaeological data can improve the reconstructing of American Indian communities and the writing of ethnohistory.

Before the 1960s, writers of Native American history literally wrote about Indians from an outsider's point of view, and they relied on printed documents as their primary evidence. When such evidence was unavailable to the writers, fabrications and imagination filled the voids to tell a good story. Since then, inventive narrative has been replaced by the writing of scholars who are applying new and various methods in analyzing American Indian history, and they are asking a wide range of questions about Indian leaders, their communities, their cultures, and so forth.

As a field, the methodology and the approach toward the history of American Indians has changed considerably. Understanding the culture of a native community and its people has become the quest of curious scholars who want to understand more about Indian life and its changing reality. And they are asking pertinent questions in a context where the printed documents that would help provide answers are limited. For example, what were the various Indian cultures like, and more precisely, how may their particular communities be reconstructed? What were their natural surroundings? How did their communities function internally? What were the elements of their infrastructures?

As scholars strive to internally analyze native communities, a variety of methodologies have been used, and new ones can be applied or combined. Categorically, several current methodologies include oral history, environ-

mental history, biographical history, ethnohistory, women's history, quantitative history, agricultural history, demographic history, and narrative his-
tory. Some works illustrate these different methodologies better than others.
Yet all of them have moved beyond narrative history, beyond simply telling
a good story.

Successful scholars like R. David Edmunds use a technique of developing
a cultural background for explaining Indian behavior and demonstrating how
Native American groups have responded. Edmunds, in both *The Potawatomis:
Keepers of the Fire* (1978) and in *The Fox Wars: The Mesquakie Challenge to
New France*, a collaboration with Joseph L. Peyser (1993), gives an account
of the cultural beginnings of these Indian communities and how their societies functioned. Other tribal histories include a similar approach, combin-
ing ethnographic data for cultural backgrounds in writing the histories of
Indian nations.

The act of Indian nations accounting for their own histories begins with
the oral tradition, thus providing an oral history of legends and myths, which
included creation stories and metaphorical tales providing for morals and
values among the people. Jan Vansina's *Oral Tradition as History* (1985) and
Donald A. Ritchie's recent *Doing Oral History* (1995) provide instruction
on how to interview people in collecting oral history and its importance. The
difficulties in collecting Indian oral history is told by a frustrated Fred
McTaggart in his insightful *Wolf that I Am: In Search of the Red Earth
People* (1976).

Helpful works have been collected and compiled in recording oral tradition, oral history, and oratory. Richard Erdoes and Alfonso Ortiz have compiled a wide range of tribal myths and legends in *American Indian Myths
and Legends* (1984). A helpful compilation is Jay Miller, *Earthmaker, Tribal
Stories from Native North America* (1992). A similar compilation with geographic representation is Terri Hardin, ed., *Legends and Lore of the American Indians* (1993). Indian oratory and commentary consisting of speeches
on a variety of subjects are in W. C. Vanderwerth, comp., *Indian Oratory:
Famous Speeches by Noted Indian Chieftains* (1971); Colin G. Calloway,
ed., *The World Turned Upside Down: Indian Voices from Early America*
(1994); Steven Mintz, *Native American Voices: A History and Anthropology* (1995); Arlene Hirschfelder, ed., *Native Heritage: Personal Accounts by
American Indians, 1790 to the Present* (1995); and in Peter Nabokov, ed.,
*Native American Testimony: A Chronicle of Indian–White Relations from
Prophecy to the Present, 1492–1992* (1992). While Calloway's and Mintz's
editions stress Indian accounts during the colonial era, Hirschfelder collected

more or less contemporary personal accounts about basic areas of life. Nabokov gives the fullest range of individual Indian perspectives, from historical leaders to contemporary spokespersons.

Related to oral tradition are works focusing on the generic Indian trickster and the Native American worldview. These insightful works include Paul Radin, *The Trickster, A Study in American Indian Mythology* (1956; repr., 1971); Howard L. Harrod, *Renewing the World: Plains Indian Religion and Morality* (1987); and Michael Kearney, *World View* (1984). The latter focuses on a model and theories about the worldviews of native communities in general around the world. A work often referred to is A. Irving Hallowell, "Ojibway Ontology, Behavior, and World View," in Stanley Diamond, ed., *Primitive Views of the World: Essays from Culture in History* (1964). To understand how legends and traditions help to explain tribal origin, Harold Courlander, *The Fourth World of the Hopis: The Epic Story of the Hopi Indians as Preserved in Their Legends and Traditions* (1971) remains a reliable narrative description and offers valuable insights into Hopi life in a surreal world.

The real world of Native American groups includes a combined reality of the physical and metaphysical. In order to comprehend this reality, one has to understand the interrelationship with plants, animals, and the spiritual dimension. These relationships of natural democracy, where all is equal among humans, animals, and plants is germane to the Indian world at the tribal level. Charlotte Erichsen-Brown, in *Medicinal and Other Uses of North American Plants: A Historical Survey with Special Reference to the Eastern Indian Tribes* (1979), provides wide scientific coverage of the role of plants, accompanying a historical survey of early observations concerning plants. A similarly helpful study is Francis Densmore's classic, *How Indians Use Wild Plants, For Food, Medicine, and Crafts* (1928; repr., 1974). Virgil J. Vogel's *American Indian Medicine* (1970) helps us realize the curing importance of plants and herbs to Indian life. To help us think about the unique roles of animals in Indian life, Calvin Martin, in *Keepers of the Game: Indian–Animal Relationships and the Fur Trade* (1978), has provoked much discussion and debate about the historic meaning of animals to Indian people.

Strong metaphorical and symbolical relationships are evident in the Mother Earth and the role of women in Native American societies. However, historians and scholars have seemingly only begun to scratch the surface in exploring the importance of gender and women's histories as means for understanding Indian history. In considering Indian women in a context with all ethnic women, the general discourse of how ethnic women have been portrayed is discussed in Antonia I. Castañeda, "Women of Color and the

Rewriting of Western History: The Discourse, Politics, and Decolonization of History" (1992). The vital role of the native woman in a Great Lakes economy is explained in Priscilla K. Buffalohead, "A Fresh Look at Ojibway Women: Farmers, Warriors, Traders" (1983). A more recent examination of the impact of missionaries on Indian women in the Great Lakes is Carol Green Devens, *Countering Colonization: Native American Women and Great Lakes Missions, 1630–1900* (1992). An early classic with much to offer about family relationships as well as a comprehensive ethnography concerning three women is Ruth Landes, *The Ojibwa Woman* (1938; repr., 1977).

Native ethos and worldview of an Indian community are closely related to the natural environment of the people. This relationship between environment and people plays a major role in the cultural history and in envisioning the circle of life for an Indian nation. For example, Christopher Vecsey and Robert W. Venables, eds., *American Indian Environments: Ecological Issues in Native American History* (1980), and J. Donald Hughes, *American Indian Ecology* (1983) have been useful in demonstrating the historical significance of American Indians to their environments. The enlightening works of Richard White, *The Roots of Dependency: Subsistence, Environment and Social Change among the Choctaws, Pawnees, and Navajos* (1983), and of William Cronon, *Changes in the Land: Indians, Colonists, and the Ecology of New England* (1983) have had critical impact in making historians and other scholars think about the important influence of natural environments on history.

As scholars study the environment–tribal relationship even more closely, the sense of a metaphysical rapport between elements of the earth, including geographic sites, flora, fauna, water, and landscape, becomes evident as disclosed in Klara Bonsack Kelley and Harris Francis, *Navajo Sacred Places* (1994). James H. Howard and Willie Lena's *Oklahoma Seminoles: Medicine, Magic, and Religion* (1984) and Howard's *Shawnee! The Ceremonialism of a Native American Tribe and Its Cultural Background* (1981) provide pertinent insights into tribal realities and their metaphysical relations.

American Indian social history and the portrayal of daily life has contributed to the historical understanding of Indian behavior. Some helpful works in this area are Royal B. Hassrick, *The Sioux: Life and Customs of a Warrior Society* (1964), and John C. Ewers, *Indian Life on the Upper Missouri* (1968). Changes in Indian social life are addressed with regard to several groups in Duane Champagne, *American Indian Societies: Strategies and Conditions of Political and Cultural Survival* (1989).

Social history has become a helpful area for understanding Native American lives and societies. By examining the society of a particular community, other important elements of Indian life become apparent. More specifically, reconstructing the infrastructure of Indian society is vitally important for understanding American Indians and their histories. Within the community, village or band, there exist important social or kindred units such as family, clan, age-group society or military society, moiety, and religious society.

The family unit, or more accurately the extended family, was the next building block in native society. Other disciplines like anthropology and sociology have been helpful in producing studies of the American Indian family unit. Studies that emphasize the importance of the family structure include Joseph H. Stauss, "The Study of American Indian Families: Implications for Applied Research" in *Family Perspective* Vol. 20, no. 4 (1986) and Robert John, "The Native American Family," in Charles H. Mindel et al., eds., *Ethnic Families in America: Patterns and Variations* (1988). Family life and clans are stressed in Bruce Trigger, *The Hurons: Farmers of the North*, 2d ed. (1990). Kindred units and Cheyenne band life are addressed in E. Adamson Hoebel, *The Cheyennes: Indians of the Great Plains*, 2d ed. (1978). Indian identity based on clans, families, and villages in the Great Lakes region are addressed in Donald L. Fixico, "The Persistence of Identity in Indian Communities of the Western Great Lakes"(1991).

Studying leadership patterns and leaders in Native American societies is synonymous with biographical history. Writing biographical history about famous Indian leaders and individuals involves solving particular problems. One concern is that because Indian leaders did not become noteworthy until adulthood, their earlier years as well as date of birth is often guesswork. Understanding the culture of the people may help a biographer describe the life of a youth of a tribe, therefore adding to the limited research information the writer may have to work with. A common trend among Native American biographies concerns their subjects' political or military relationship with the United States. Usually, their careers conflicted with American political or military leaders.

Helpful biographies of Indian leaders include R. David Edmunds, *Tecumseh and the Quest for Indian Leadership* (1984), and his biography of Tecumseh's counterpart, *The Shawnee Prophet* (1983). Early biographical classics that established this method of understanding Indian history are Stanley Vestal, *Sitting Bull: Champion of the Sioux* (1932; repr., 1957); Mari Sandoz, *Crazy Horse: The Strange Man of the Oglalas* (1942; repr., 1961); Helen Addison Howard, *Saga of Chief Joseph* (1941; repr., 1978); and Angie Debo, *Geronimo: The Man, His Time, His Place* (1976). Other well-done biographies could be listed, if space were not a problem. Two biographical anthologies helpful in understanding Indian leadership in communities are R. David Edmunds, ed.,

American Indian Leaders: Studies in Diversity (1980), and L. G. Moses and Raymond Wilson, eds., *Indian Lives: Essays on Nineteenth- and Twentieth-Century Native American Leaders* (1985).

Rarely are native women viewed by scholars for their common role in making medicine as shamans and as leaders in society. A helpful brief biography is David E. Jones, ed., *Sanapia: Comanche Medicine Woman* (1972), and an early classic is Frank B. Linderman, ed., *Red Mother* (1932), published later as *Pretty-shield, Medicine Woman of the Crows* (1972). A compilation of most of the literature on Indian women is found in the helpful book of Gretchen M. Bataille and Kathleen Mullen Sands, *American Indian Women Telling Their Lives* (1984).

Personal narratives and native autobiographies have provided extra insight into the lives of historical Indian figures and/or their communities. The classic *Black Elk Speaks* (1932), edited by John Neihardt, has set an important precedent for other personal accounts in providing a shaman's perspective. A similar successful work is John Lame Deer and Richard Erdoes, *Lame Deer, Seeker of Visions* (1972). Indian autobiographies are usually assisted by writers, and these works, which provide valuable insight into the leadership and the history of the Native American communities, include Donald Jackson, ed., *Black Hawk: An Autobiography* (1955). Selected autobiographies of Indian women are Maria Campbell, *Halfbreed* (1973; repr., 1982); Ruth Underhill, ed., *Papago Woman* [Maria Chona] (1979); Crying Wind, *Crying Wind* (1977); Beverly Hungry Wolf, *The Ways of My Grandmothers* (1980); Nancy Oestreich Lurie, ed., *Mountain Wolf Woman, Sister of Crashing Thunder: The Autobiography of a Winnebago Indian* (1961); Vada R. Carlson, ed., *No Turning Back: A True Account of a Hopi Girl's Struggle to Bridge the Gap between the World of Her People and the World of the White Man* (1964); and Mary Crow Dog, with Richard Erdoes, *Lakota Woman* (1990).

First encounters, or contact histories, usually apply a comparative analysis, and have helped to lay a foundation for studying Native Americans as a people with various cultures, thereby dismissing the gross stereotype that all Indians are the same. Beginning with Francis Jennings, *The Invasion of America: Indians, Colonialism, and the Cant of Conquest* (1975), ethnohistory has played a dual role as a field and a methodology in illustrating the depth of Native American groups as a people with various cultures. One ethnohistorian who has been prolific is James Axtell, author of *The European and the Indian: Essays in the Ethnohistory of Colonial North America* (1981), *The Invasion Within: The Contest of Cultures in Colonial North America* (1985), *After Columbus: Essays in the Ethnohistory of Co-*

lonial of Colonial North America (1988), and *Beyond 1492: Encounters of Colonial North America* (1992).

Economic history represents another kind of discipline and approach for understanding Native Americans and their communities. Accepting the fact that subsistence is economic history for Native Americans, Indian groups practiced horticulture, agriculture, and hunting and gathering. Ron Trosper has challenged scholars to consider economic history as a means for understanding American Indian history, in "That Other Discipline: Economics and American Indian History," in Colin G. Calloway, ed., *New Directions in American Indian History* (1988). A large work comprised of a dozen different scholars stressing Indian economics is John H. Moore, ed., *The Political Economy of North American Indians* (1993). A general survey of Indian agriculture, R. Douglas Hurt's *Indian Agriculture in America: Prehistory to the Present* (1987) demonstrates that for many native groups, much of Indian life focused on raising crops. One work that integrates environmental analysis and agricultural history is David Lewis, *Neither Wolf Nor Dog: American Indians, Environment, Agrarian Change* (1994), an ethnohistorical comparisons of three groups—Ute, Tohono O'odom, and Hupa.

The challenge of writing American Indian history has inspired scholars to reconsider the previous portrayals of Indian people. Stereotypes and previous histories have misrepresented Native Americans, as stated by Laurence Hauptman, in *Tribes and Tribulations: Misconceptions about American Indians and Their Histories* (1995). Calvin Martin's collection of essays by various scholars addressing various aspects of Native American history is *The American Indian and the Problem of History* (1987). In his own singular effort, Martin called for a rethinking of American Indian history, in *In the Spirit of the Earth: Rethinking History and Time* (1992). Instead of seeing Indian history as a problem, Colin Calloway has chosen to view the field as an opportunity for new ways of conceiving and writing history, as illustrated by various authors in his edited book, *New Directions in American Indian History*.

In summarizing the various studies about Native American history and the kinds of methodologies in their approach, the works mentioned in this essay constitute only a selection. Other works not mentioned are also indicative of these methodologies in which American Indian history is being analyzed differently and reconstructed, and an apology is offered to these authors for the fact that space here was too limited to allow inclusion of all of their works.

Scholars have successfully used a cross-cultural approach in studying American Indians. On the whole, they have examined the dynamics of exchange and interaction between the United States government and the Indian nations, such as federal Indian policy, or treaty making, trade, councils, and war. Analyzing Indian behavior in history, according to cultural influences, involves contact history, oral history, social history, environmental history, agricultural history perhaps, economic history, policy history, and military history. Additional helpful sources of data and research are geography, cartography, demography, psychology, and linguistics for cross-disciplinary approaches.

Generally, ethnohistory has been an effective approach for understanding Native American history. The current trend in studying Native American history includes ethnographic data and cultural history. Scholars are examining Native American communities, and the ways in which these communities have responded to key historical events. This might be considered behavioral analysis, but in essence such study has focused on how Indians and whites have differed culturally in learning about the general history of the interactions of the two races. Richard White's *The Middle Ground: Indians, Empires, and Republics in the Great Lakes Region, 1650–1815* (1991) has served as a model for how Native American groups, Europeans, and Americans have created history together. Such inclusive studies of Indian communities examine ethnographic data and incorporate it into more complete historical analysis, such as James H. Merrell's *The Indian's New World: Catawbas and Their Neighbors from European Contact through the Era of Removal* (1989) and Gregory Dowd's *A Spirited Resistance: The North American Indian Struggle for Unity, 1745–1815* (1992).

What new directions is American Indian history taking, and what is its potential? These are intellectually challenging questions, and at least two directions can be immediately identified.

One direction involves more contemporary topics. As this century comes to an end, much needs to be done about twentieth- century Native American history. The possible subjects are numerous, ranging form federal Indian policies, tribal histories since 1900, economic history (including, for example, that of Indian gaming), urban history, and studies focusing on specific issues and problems. Such issues and problems might include fishing, hunting, cultural, and legal rights. Sovereignty, self-determination, and modern cultural communities are other areas.

The second direction is a closer examination of Indian communities, which involves scholars in historically reconstructing native communities. An internal analysis of communities can reestablish infrastructure of Indian societies for certain time periods. Theoretically, this would ideally involve the totality of an Indian community in examining oral tradition, cultural values, environmental relation, societal norms, kinship patterns, leadership and governance, metaphysical relations, and the ethos of the people.

In order to better understand Indian history, germane questions need to be raised about Native American communities, their leaders, and their realities. Too often, historians use their own sense of reality as a basis for writing about Indian history. This external interpretation by an outsider writing Indian history should not be accepted as the historical truth, nor should this genre of history be accepted as award-winning history. Remembering that the foci of history are not the same for everyone helps to determine the point of perspective from which history is viewed, and to verify the claim that one's perception of reality influences one's understanding of history. Observational history is one dimensional and limited to description, whereas a fuller understanding of American Indian history requires rethinking the Indian past as distinct communities with their own cultures and with their own historical relationships with other cultures and Indian communities.

Bibliography

Axtell, James, *The European and the Indian: Essays in the Ethnohistory of Colonial North America*. New York: Oxford University Press, 1981.

——. *The Invasion Within: The Contest of Cultures in Colonial North America*. New York: Oxford University Press, 1985.

——. *After Columbus: Essays in the Ethnohistory of Colonial of Colonial North America*. New York: Oxford University Press, 1988.

——. *Beyond 1492: Encounters of Colonial North America*. New York: Oxford University Press, 1992.

Bataille, Gretchen M., and Kathleen Mullen Sands. *American Indian Women Telling Their Lives*. Lincoln: Bison Books, 1984.

Berkhofer, Robert F., Jr. "The Political Context of a New Indian History." *Pacific Historical Review* 40:3 (August 1971), 357–82.

Buffalohead, Priscilla K. "A Fresh Look at Ojibway Women: Farmers, Warriors, Traders." *Minnesota History* 48 (Summer 1983), 236–44.

Calloway, Colin G., ed. *New Directions in American Indian History*. Norman: University of Oklahoma Press, 1988.

——. *The World Turned Upside Down: Indian Voices from Early America*. Boston and New York: Beford Books, 1994.

Campbell, Maria. *Halfbreed*. Toronto: McClelland and Stewart, 1973; repr. 1982.

Carlson, Vada., ed. [About Qoyawayma, Polingaysi (Elizabeth Q. White)] *No Turning Back: A True Account of a Hopi Girl's Struggle to Bridge the Gap between the World of Her People and the World of the White Man*. Albuquerque: University of New Mexico Press, 1964.

Castañeda, Antonia L. "Women of Color and the Rewriting of Western History:

The Discourse, Politics, and Decolonization of History." *Pacific Historical Review* 61 (November 1992), 501-34.

Champagne, Duane. *American Indian Societies: Strategies and Conditions of Political and Cultural Survival*. Cambridge: Cultural Survival, 1989.

Courlander, Harold. *The Fourth World of the Hopis: The Epic Story of the Hopi Indians as Preserved in their Legends and Traditions*. 6th ed. Albuquerque: University of New Mexico Press, 1994.

Cronon, William. *Changes in the Land: Indians, Colonists, and the Ecology of New England*. New York: Hill and Wang, 1983.

Crow Dog, Mary, with Richard Erdoes. *Lakota Woman*. New York: Grove Weidenfeld, 1990.

Crying Wind. *Crying Wind*. Chicago: Moody Press, 1977.

Debo, Angie. *Geronimo: The Man, His Time, His Place*. Norman: University of Oklahoma Press, 1976.

Densmore, Francis. *How Indians Use Wild Plants, For Food, Medicine, and Crafts*. New York: Dover Publications, 1974. (Originally *Uses of Plants by the Chippewa Indians*, Forty-Fourth Annual Report of the Bureau of American Ethnology, 1928.)

Devens, Carol. *Countering Colonization: Native American Women and Great Lakes Missions, 1630–1900*. Berkeley: University of California Press, 1992.

Diamond, Stanley., ed. *Primitive Views of the World: Essays from Culture in History*. New York: Columbia University Press, 1964.

Dowd, Gregory. *A Spirited Resistance: The North American Indian Struggle for Unity, 1745–1815*. Baltimore: Johns Hopkins University Press, 1992.

Edmunds, R. David, and Joseph Peyser. *The Fox Wars: The Mesquakie Challenge to New France*. Norman: University of Oklahoma Press, 1993.

Edmunds, R. David., ed. *American Indian Leaders: Studies in Diversity*. Lincoln: University of Nebraska Press, 1980.

———. *The Potawatomis: Keepers of the Fire*. Norman: University of Oklahoma Press, 1978.

———. *The Shawnee Prophet*. Lincoln: University of Nebraska Press, 1983.

———. *Tecumseh and the Quest for Indian Leadership*. Boston: Little, Brown and Company, 1984.

Erdoes, Richard, and Alfonso Ortiz, eds. *American Indian Myths and Legends*. New York: Pantheon Books, 1984.

Erichsen-Brown, Charlotte. *Medicinal and Other Uses of North American Plants: A Historical Survey with Special Reference to the Eastern Indian Tribes*. Aurora, Ontario: Breezy Creek Press, 1979.

Ewers, John C. *Indian Life on the Upper Missouri*. Norman: University of Oklahoma Press, 1968.

Fenton, William N. "Ethnohistory and Its Problems." *Ethnohistory* 9:1 (Winter 1962), 1–23.

Fixico, Donald L. "The Persistence of Identity in Indian Communities of the Western Great Lakes." *Ethnicity and Public Policy* 9 (1991), 109–48.

Forbes, Jack D. "The Historian and the Indian: Racial Bias in American History."

The Americas 19:4 (April 1963), 349–62.

———. "Frontiers in American History and The Role of the Frontier Historian." *Ethnohistory* 15:2 (Spring 1968), 203–35.

Haan, Richard L. "Another Example of Stereotypes on the Early American Frontier: The Imperialist Historians and the American Indian." *Ethnohistory* 20:2 (Spring 1973), 143–52.

Hardin, Terri., ed. *Legends and Lore of the American Indians*. New York: Barnes and Noble Books, 1993.

Harrod, Howard L. *Renewing the World: Plains Indian Religion and Morality*. Tucson: University of Arizona Press, 1987.

Hassrick, Royal B. *The Sioux: Life and Customs of a Warrior Society*. Norman: University of Oklahoma Press, 1964.

Hauptman, Laurence M. *Tribes and Tribulations: Misconceptions about American Indians and Their Histories*. Albuquerque: University of New Mexico Press, 1995.

Hirschfelder, Arlene, ed. *Native Heritage: Personal Accounts by American Indians, 1790 to the Present*. New York: Macmillan, 1995.

Hoebel, E. Adamson. *The Cheyennes: Indians of the Great Plains*. 2d ed. Fort Worth et al.: Holt, Rinehart and Winston, 1978.

Howard, Helen Addison. *Saga of Chief Joseph*. Caxton, Idaho: Caxton Printers, 1941; repr., 1978.

Howard, James H. *Shawnee! The Ceremonialism of a Native American Tribe and Its Cultural Background*. Athens: Ohio University Press, 1981.

Howard, James H., and Willie Lena. *Oklahoma Seminoles: Medicine, Magic, and Religion*. Norman: University of Oklahoma Press, 1984.

Hughes, J. Donald. *American Indian Ecology*. El Paso: Texas Western Press, 1983.

Hungry Wolf, Beverly. *The Ways of My Grandmothers*. New York: William Morrow and Co., 1980.

Hurt, R. Douglas. *Indian Agriculture in America: Prehistory to the Present*. Lawrence: University of Kansas Press, 1987.

Jackson, Donald. *Black Hawk: An Autobiography*. Urbana: University of Illinois Press, 1955; repr., 1964.

Jacobs, Wilbur R. "The Indian and the Frontier in American History—A Need for Revision." *The Western Historical Quarterly* 7:1 (January 1973), 43–56.

Jennings, Francis. *The Invasion of America: Indians, Colonialism, and the Cant of Conquest*. New York: W. W. Norton and Company, 1975.

———. "A Growing Partnership: Historians, Anthropologists, and American Indian History." *The History Teacher* 14:1 (November 1980), 87–104.

Johnson, Jay K., ed. *The Development of Southeastern Archaeology*. Tuscaloosa and London: University of Alabama Press, 1993.

Jones, David E., ed. *Sanapia: Comanche Medicine Woman*. New York: Holt, Rinehart and Winston, 1972.

Kearney, Michael. *World View*. Novato, Calif.: Chandler and Sharp Publishers, 1984.

Kelley, Klara Bonsack, and Harris Francis. *Navajo Sacred Places*. Bloomington:

Indiana University Press, 1994.

Lame Deer, John (Fire), and Richard Erdoes. *Lame Deer, Seeker of Visions*. New York: Touchstone, 1972.

Landes, Ruth. *The Ojibwa Woman*. New York: Columbia University Press, 1938; repr. 1977.

Lewis, David. *Neither Wolf Nor Dog: American Indians, Environment, and Agrarian Change*. New York: Oxford University Press, 1994.

Linderman, Frank B. *Pretty-shield, Medicine Woman of the Crows*. Lincoln: University of Nebraska Press, 1972. (Originally *Red Mother*, 1932.)

Lurie, Nancy Oestreich. *Mountain Wolf Woman, Sister of Crashing Thunder: The Autobiography of a Winnebago Indian* Ann Arbor: University of Michigan Press, 1961.

McTaggart, Fred. *Wolf that I Am: In Search of the Red Earth People*. Boston: Houghton Mifflin, 1976; repr., Norman: University of Oklahoma Press, 1984.

Martin, Calvin, ed. *The American Indian and the Problem of History*. New York: Oxford University Press, 1987.

———. "Ethnohistory: A Better Way to Write Indian History." *The Western Historical Quarterly* 9:1 (January 1978), 41–56.

———. *Keepers of the Game: Indian–Animal Relationships and the Fur Trade*. Berkeley and Los Angeles: University of California Press, 1978.

———. *In the Spirit of the Earth: Rethinking History and Time*. Baltimore: Johns Hopkins University Press, 1992.

Merrell, James H. *The Indian's New World: Catawbas and Their Neighbors from European Contact through the Era of Removal*. Chapel Hill: University of North Carolina Press, 1989.

Miller, Jay, ed. *Earthmaker, Tribal Stories from Native North America*. New York: Perigree Books, 1992.

Mindel, Charles H., Robert W. Habenstein, and Roosevelt Wright, Jr., eds., *Ethnic Families in America: Patterns and Variations*. 3d ed. New York: Elsevier, 1988.

Mintz, Steven. *Native American Voices: A History and Anthropology*. St. James, N.Y.: Brandywine Press, 1995.

Moore, John H., ed. *The Political Economy of North American Indians*. Norman: University of Oklahoma Press, 1993.

Moses, L. G., and Raymond Wilson, eds. *Indian Lives: Essays on Nineteenth- and Twentieth-Century Native American Leaders*. Albuquerque: University of New Mexico Press, 1985.

Nabokov, Peter, ed. *Native American Testimony: A Chronicle of Indian–White Relations from Prophecy to the Present, 1492–1992*. New York: Penguin Books, 1992.

Neihardt, John G., ed. *Black Elk Speaks: Being the Life Story of a Holy Man of the Oglala Sioux*. New York: Pocket Books, 1973.

Olson, James C. "Some Reflections on Historical Method and Indian History." *Ethnohistory* 5:1 (Winter 1958), 48–59.

Pargellis, Stanley. "The Problem of American Indian History." *Ethnohistory* 4:2 (Spring 1957), 113–24.

Radin, Paul. *The Trickster: A Study in American Indian Mythology*. New York: Schocken Books, 1971.

Ritchie, Donald A. *Doing Oral History*. New York: Twayne Publishers, 1995.

Sandoz, Mari. *Crazy Horse: The Strange Man of the Oglalas*. Hastings House, 1942; repr., 1961.

Stauss, Joseph (Jay) H. "The Study of American Indian Families: Implications for Applied Research." *Family Perspective* 20:4 (1986), 337–52.

Trigger, Bruce. *The Hurons: Farmers of the North*. 2d ed. Fort Worth et al.: Holt, Rinehart and Winston, 1990.

Underhill, Ruth, ed. *Papago Woman* [Maria Chona]. New York: Holt, Rinehart and Winston, 1979.

Vanderwerth, W. C., comp. *Indian Oratory: Famous Speeches by Noted Indian Chieftains*. Norman: University of Oklahoma Press, 1971.

Vansina, Jan. *Oral Tradition as History*. Madison: University of Wisconsin Press, 1985.

Vecsey, Christopher, and Robert W. Venables, eds. *American Indian Environments: Ecological Issues in Native American History*. Syracuse, N.Y.: Syracuse University Press, 1980.

Vestal, Stanley. *Sitting Bull: Champion of the Sioux*. Boston: Houghton Mifflin Company, 1932; repr., 1957.

Vogel, Virgil J. *American Indian Medicine*. Norman: University of Oklahoma Press, 1970.

Washburn, Wilcomb E. "A Moral History of Indian–White Relations: Needs and Opportunities for Study," *Ethnohistory* 4:1 (Winter 1957), 47–61.

White, Richard. *The Roots of Dependency: Subsistence, Environment, and Social Change among the Choctaws, Pawnees, and Navajos*. Lincoln: University of Nebraska Press, 1983.

―――. *The Middle Ground: Indians, Empires, and Republics in the Great Lakes Region, 1650–1815*. Cambridge: Cambridge University Press, 1991.

Contributors

JAMES AXTELL is Kenan Professor of Humanities in history at the College of William and Mary. He has received numerous awards and grants acknowledging his scholarship, including a Guggenheim Fellowship and awards for outstanding faculty. His many publications include *The European and the Indian: Essays in the Ethnohistory of Colonial North America* (1981); *The Invasion Within: The Contest of Cultures in Colonial North America* (1985); *After Columbus: Essays in the Ethnohistory of Colonial North America* (1988); and *Beyond 1492: Encounters in Colonial North America* (1992).

WILLIAM T. HAGAN is Professor of History at the University of Oklahoma. He was instrumental in establishing the field of American Indian history with his book *American Indians*. His other books include *The Indian in American History; Indian Police and Judges: Experiments in Acculturation and Control; The Indian Rights Association: The Herbert Welsh Years, 1882–1904; Quanah Parker, Comanche Chief; The Sac and Fox Indians*; and *United States–Comanche Relations: The Reservation Years*. He is the past president of the American Society for Ethnohistory and of the Western History Association, the latter of which he helped to found.

GLENDA RILEY is Alexander M. Bracken Professor of History at Ball State University in Muncie, Indiana. She is the author of numerous books and articles regarding women in the American West, including *Frontierswomen: The Iowa Experience; The Female Frontier, A Place to Grow: Women in the American West; Women and Indians on the Frontier; The Life and Legacy of Annie Oakley*; and *Building and Breaking Families in the American West*. Riley is also the recipient of numerous awards and honors, including a Distinguished Fulbright and a Huntington Library Fellowship; and she is a member of the Iowa Women's Hall of Fame. She is currently a past president of the Western History Association.

THEDA PERDUE is Professor of History at the University of Kentucky. She has been a visiting professor at the University of Auckland and at the University of North Carolina. Her honors and awards are numerous, and she has edited or coedited five books, including *Nations Remembered: An Oral History of the Five Civilized Tribes, 1865–1907* (1980); *Cherokee Editor: The Writings of Elias Boudinot* (1983); and *The Cherokee Removal: A Brief History with Documents* (1995). She has also authored *Native Carolinians: The Indians of North Carolina* (1985); and *Slavery and the Evolution of Cherokee Society, 1540–1866* (1987).

RICHARD WHITE is McCleland Professor of History at the University of Washington. Among his awards are a Guggenheim Fellowship and a MacArthur Grant (1995), as well as several writing awards. He has served as the president of the Western History Association and has authored *Land Use, Environment, and Social Change: The Shaping of Island County, Island County, Washington, 1790–1940* (1980); *The Roots of Dependency: Subsistence, Environment, and Social Change among the Choctaws, Pawnees and Navajos* (1983); *It's Your Misfortune and None of My Own: A History of the American West* (1991); and *The Middle Ground: Indians, Empires, and Republics in the Great Lakes Region, 1650–1815* (1991).

ANGELA CAVENDER WILSON has completed her course work for the doctorate in history at Cornell University. She has taught at Ithaca College, and she is working on her dissertation, an oral historical study, whose working title is "A Dakota Way of Life and Culture and Philosophy." She has been awarded an Andrew Mellon Foundation Award; a Special Minorities Fellowship; and a Sage Fellowship, and she received an honorable mention for a Ford Foundation Predoctoral Fellowship. She has presented papers at the Native Women Historians: Challenges and Issues Conference, held at Southwest State University; at the Western History Association Conference; and at other conferences.

DONALD L. FIXICO is Professor of History at Western Michigan University, Kalamazoo. He has written numerous articles and is the author of *Termination and Relocation: Federal Indian Policy, 1945–1960*; and *Urban Indians*; and is the editor of *An Anthology of Western Great Lakes Indian History*. Fixico has been a visiting lecturer and visiting professor at several universities, and he has taught abroad at the University of Nottingham, England. His research interests focus on Native Americans in the nineteenth and twentieth centuries.

Index